HAPPINESS
Anywhere Anytime

Happiness secrets revealed
by a hitman, missing socks,
and my dog

Bruce Wells, Ph.D.

ε

Eudaimonia BJ Books
Melbourne, Australia

First published in Australia 2014

ISBN-10: 1500700509
ISBN-13: 978-1500700508

Typeset in 11/16 Garamond.

Published by Eudaimonia BJ Books Australia 2014

Dedication

To my mother who has taught me much about happiness through her
unconditional love and never-ending support.

Contents

Chapter 4   Live a Fully Connected Life

PART TWO

Practice Happiness

Your Happier Life
Starts Now!

Mike is 52. He's still waiting to be happy. He hoped he'd be happy in his 30s after deciding on following in his father's footsteps and becoming an engineer in his 20s. Then he expected to be happy in his 40s after gaining promotions, marrying a beautiful woman, and starting a family in his 30s. And he was certain he'd be happy once he reached 50 after becoming a senior manager, paying off the mortgage and with his two kids about to finish high school. He'd done all the right things. He'd checked all the boxes. Why was he still not happy?

Mike's story is remarkably common today with more and more people complaining of not being happy. At the same time the rates of people suffering from depression, becoming addicted to drugs or alcohol, and contemplating suicide are higher than ever before. All of this in western countries where we have been blessed with better medical care, greater access to education, improved living conditions, more disposable income, and increased leisure time. So why aren't we all blissfully happy? What's going on?

What is Happiness?

I believe that the answer to this question lies in the definition of the word happiness. The most popular meaning of the word is associated with fleeting pleasurable feelings that come from *getting* something such as getting good sex, delicious chocolate, a new car, a boss' praise at work, a bargain at the end-of-year sales. This is the definition that we are sold by the consumer-driven society in which we live. Whenever we catch the train to work, surf the internet, or lounge in front of the TV we are constantly bombarded with a blitzkrieg of advertising and the message is clear: "Get this product and you will be happy." Consequently, this first definition has us believing that happiness is something outside of ourselves, something that is always 'out there'. And so we spend time, money and effort chasing it. If only we can marry the right person, buy the right product, get the right job promotion, live in the right neighborhood, or visit the right Buddhist monastery then we will be happy.

In contrast, the second definition of happiness is concerned with more enduring feelings of happiness involving contentment, fulfillment, and peacefulness. Here the focus is on *being* such as being true to one's values and one's strengths, being immersed in the moment, being grateful for one's blessings, and being part of a worthwhile cause that is larger than oneself. Whereas the first type of happiness is momentary and is reliant upon us receiving favorable reactions from others or being able to get things, the second form of happiness is more enduring and fulfilling because *it is generated from within us*. While both forms of happiness are certainly important and are to be enjoyed in life, it is this second richer and more stable form of happiness that is the focus of this book.

Before we move on there is one other ingredient of happiness that must be mentioned. In the field of wellness we make the distinction between the absence of illness and health. Being free of disease does not mean you are healthy. Being healthy is the result of intentional healthy living practices such as regular exercise, a good food plan, the proper amount of sleep, being a non-smoker, and drinking minimal alcohol. Similarly, being free of *un*happiness does not mean you are happy. We can all testify to days or weeks when we weren't unhappy or miserable but we certainly weren't jumping over the moon with joy either.

The point? If you seek true happiness you have to be proactive and embrace a lifetime of happiness-promoting practices. This book will show you how.

Happiness Anywhere Anytime

My interest in the topic of happiness and in providing people with strategies to be happier has evolved from three main sources: (1) my wellness coaching practice where clients take responsibility for making purposeful behavioral changes in their lives believing that they possess all the tools within themselves to succeed; (2) the growing field of positive psychology which maintains that by cultivating a person's positive emotions he or she can be more productive, open-minded, creative, and caring, and enjoy a happier life; and (3) the field of emotional wellness where people learn how to be emotionally resilient by taking responsibility for their own emotions, by practicing optimism, and by responding to challenges as opportunities.

All of these approaches have a lot in common with respect to improving an individual's happiness. In particular, all three emphasize the importance of using one's strengths, adopting a positive outlook, being in the moment, and practicing a sense of community. Consequently, these four concepts represent the foundation blocks of the Happiness Anywhere Anytime program. And the cement that binds the blocks together is knowing, and believing, that the potential for happiness resides within you…anywhere anytime.

I have divided the program into two parts. Part 1 contains four chapters of stories – the happiness secrets. The first three chapters contain secrets devoted to developing your immediate self, while the fourth chapter's secrets influence how you interact with others. Part 2 contains activities allowing you to practice the happiness secrets. Here is an overview of the program.

Step 1:   Live from the Inside Out

Being the person you are meant to be and living with greater passion by aligning your values, strengths, and life purpose with your daily behaviors.

Step 2:   Live with a Positive Attitude

Seeing the world with a sunny confident outlook that is optimistic and highly resilient to both change and adversity.

Step 3:   Live in the Present

Savoring the moment – the birthplace of happiness – by remaining young at heart, expressing gratitude, and laughing more.

Step 4:   Live a Fully Connected Life

Enjoying more meaningful and fulfilling relationships through enhanced communication, helping others, seeing the best in others, and being more compassionate.

Together, all four steps will allow you to take complete control of your own happiness by showing you how to more effectively tap into the incredible resources that you already have within you while also helping you make the most of your current circumstances. Now let's look at each of these sections in more detail.

Step 1:   Live from the Inside Out

Ever been to a party and found that you felt out of sorts all night? You tried so hard to have a good time and to fit in but something was just not right. You couldn't seem to be yourself. You looked around at all the happy faces and concluded that the problem must be with you. Most troubling of all is that this same feeling seems to shadow you most of your waking hours. What does it mean?

From the moment we are born our parents, our schools, our workplaces, and our society are all urging us to fit in, to do the right thing. At the same time everywhere we look we are confronted with images of people who are better looking, fitter, richer, smarter, more successful, or more famous than we are. Under this relentless assault it's hardly surprising that we stop celebrating our uniqueness and become conditioned into comparing ourselves with others as a gauge of our success, and ultimately, our happiness. And in trying to conform to society's definition of success we gradually lose touch with what is truly important to us, to our personal strengths, and to our passion or calling.

Unsure of who we really are or what we should be doing with our lives we resign ourselves into a malaise of 'settling'. We settle for that job that we know doesn't allow us to use our strengths or unleash our passion but hey, it's a secure job, so it will do. We settle for the husband or wife who we know we don't connect with at a deeper level but hey, it's better than spending nights alone, so he or she will do. We settle for a life of mediocre happiness because the thought of having to put our emotions on the line when confronting our true selves and our untapped potential just too darn terrifying. So we choose to play it safe and have a near-life experience instead of being true to ourselves and experiencing unlimited happiness.

'Live from the Inside Out' will show you how to reconnect with your inner true self. Here is where you will discover what is most important to you, your set of values, which is your built-in compass towards a happier life. When your daily actions and behaviors are aligned with your values you experience less inner conflict resulting in less illness, less stress, more effective decision-making abilities, and more happiness. All those nagging gut feelings of doubt and indecision are replaced with feelings of certainty and assurance.

In this section you will also identify your strengths, an integral component of living authentically. We spend far too much of our time, especially in the workplace, sweating over our weaknesses trying to mould them into something workable. For greater happiness – as well as increased motivation, creativity, and productivity – we should be spending most of our time honing our strengths and following our passion.

The final aspect of living from the inside out concerns living a meaningful life where we feel that we are contributing to something larger than ourselves. In an era of rampant individualism obsessed with personal gratification, it is extraordinary, and very revealing, how people come together as one at times of national tragedy or during natural disasters. A sense of meaning is suddenly given to people's lives and they respond magnificently. At such times we show our very best selves. Because of the awesome potential power that our values, strengths, and our hunger for a life of meaning have in shaping our lives this is considered the most important section for developing an enduring happiness.

Step 2:   Live with a Positive Attitude

When people are asked the question, "What would have to happen for you to become very happy?" many respond with either "I'd have to win something" or "I'd have to be in the right place at the right time." They are referring to luck or circumstances, both of which allow them to wash their hands of any responsibility for their own happiness. They see life as a game of chance where they have no option but to wait till their perfect soul mate knocks on their front door, till head hunters chase them down with that once-in-a-lifetime job opportunity, or till they win the lottery. In this scenario our feelings are like leaves on a windy day blown about willy-nilly by whatever circumstances life throws our way. We have no influence over our own happiness.

Fortunately, we now know that this is not the case. In the field of psychology, cognitive-behavioral therapy shows us that the way we *think* about our life circumstances and the way we *interpret* situations determines our emotional and behavioral responses. We have complete control over our emotions and how we react to things. We see this illustrated in the workplace when two men have completely different reactions after missing out on promotions – one man becomes disheartened, retreats into a shell, and his performance deteriorates while another man is re-motivated, becomes more of a team player, and pursues further professional development.

What is so exciting is realizing that the men's contrasting attitudes – one positive, the other negative – are learned. Negative self-defeating attitudes are simply the result of conditioned fears and doubts and like all habits can be unlearned. And positive motivating attitudes that energize and excite you and which propel you towards your goals can be learned. So by changing your thoughts and the way you react to situations you will change your feelings and behaviors.

This is a monumental fact because it means that your happiness is only ever just one thought away. Like trying to tune into the wavelength of a radio station once you know how to tune into your own emotions feelings of happiness will always be within your grasp, no matter the situation, no matter the circumstances. 'Live with a Positive Attitude' will show you how to accomplish this.

This section will also show you how to replace negative attitudes with positive attitudes. Armed with positive attitudes your entire life will change for the better. As well as feeling happier you will be more confident and optimistic, and feel less stressed and more relaxed. Also, with a positive attitude you will always be able to make the best of your prevailing circumstances instead of waiting for the ideal circumstances, and you will enjoy more success in your career and in your relationships.

Step 3:   Live in the Present

One of the myths we have fallen victim to in our quest for greater happiness is thinking that happiness is a destination. In doing this we have set our happiness as a point on the horizon that we have to reach. How often have you heard, or perhaps, said yourself, the following phrase, "I'll be happy when….I get a job promotion, can afford a home theatre system, quit smoking, get married, pay off the mortgage, lose 10 kg"? This is an illusion because once we reach our goal (assuming we do) we immediately replace it with another goal on the horizon. Happiness becomes a tantalizing carrot that is forever out of reach, a feeling that only exists in the future. But happiness is only possible in the now – you can't save it up till your next long weekend comes along, or defer it till you're less busy, or cash it in when you're feeling miserable.

We deprive ourselves of experiencing happiness in the present in other ways too. We have become busy-addicts – busy checking our smartphones for text messages during conversations, busy snapping photos and selfies wherever we go, busy eating lunch while reading emails and surfing the internet at work. We're constantly on the move like bees in a flower bed flitting from one activity to the next. We're afraid that if we stop even for a moment we'll miss an opportunity to experience true happiness. But we're so busy *chasing* happiness we don't give ourselves the chance to stop and *feel* happiness.

We also spend a lot of our time dwelling over past regrets or worrying needlessly about future events that will never happen. This is what causes most of our stress and anxiety. And takes our attention away from the present where happiness is to be found. However, as you will remember from the previous section, if our thoughts, which direct our emotions, are concerned with what we are doing in the present moment it is impossible to feel stressed.

'Live in the Present' will show you how to be happier and less stressed by aligning your thoughts with your physical body (which funnily enough is always in the present). You will learn to savor the journey. This section will also help you relearn the child skill of being totally absorbed in one activity in the moment. By being able to fully immerse yourself in the moment whenever you choose you will be rewarded with greater feelings of relaxation, clarity of vision, contentment, and increased productivity.

Step 4:   Live a Fully Connected Life

Evidence for the beneficial impact of meaningful relationships on happiness is clear cut. The greater the quality of relationship between friends or between romantic partners the greater the happiness. Similarly, happiness rises with participation in charity organizations and with membership and social involvement in recreation clubs. Connecting meaningfully with others contributes to greater happiness, fewer health problems, less stress, and increased cognitive functioning.

However, many people today are suffering from a lack of quality social and romantic interactions for a variety of reasons. Chief among them is the fact that we are not giving ourselves enough opportunities to experience casual face-to-face interactions. The rise in the number of people living alone, our love affair with personal technology, the tendency of more and more people to work from home, and a world switched into overdrive has meant that people are finding it increasingly difficult to develop new friendships. Gone are the days when everyone knew their neighbors and when face-to-face talks were the standard way of conducting conversations.

'Live a Fully Connected Life' addresses this worrying trend by providing you with the tools to both improve your ability to start new friendships and to further enrich your existing social and romantic relationships. By mastering enhanced communication skills, displaying greater empathy and compassion for others and through practicing regular acts of service towards your fellow man you will be blessed with greater feelings of self-love, peacefulness, and happiness.

The Ten Rules of Happiness Anywhere Anytime

This book is based on 10 rules. To gain the most benefit from the book it is important you keep these rules uppermost in your mind while reading The Happiness Secrets stories and when doing the Practice Happiness activities. You may like to copy them on to post-it notes and stick them on your computer screen, beside your bed, or on your car's dashboard. You want them to become your happiness mantras.

1. The potential for happiness is within you....*anywhere anytime.*
2. Happiness is the consequence of living from the inside out, living with a positive attitude, living in the present, and living a fully connected life.
3. You are responsible for your own happiness.
4. Happiness is *a skill,* and so, can be learnt.
5. You *deserve* to be happy.
6. You have to want to be happy.
7. You have to decide to be happy.
8. Your feelings of happiness are only felt in the *now.*
9. Everyone wants to be happy.
10. Happiness is a lifetime project.

How to Make Sure this Book Radically Changes your Life

Despite a wealth of books being written about happiness few seem to offer practical and academic jargon-free advice for being happier. And as a former primary school teacher, tour guide and long-time motivation speaker experience has shown me time and time again the incredible learning value of every day stories relevant to one's audience. With this in mind I set out to develop a book that would be half storybook, half workbook.

The first part of the book, Happiness Secrets, is a collection of short stories designed to pique your interest in the secrets necessary for achieving greater happiness. I do not claim to have 'discovered' these secrets. All the secrets are well-researched and commonly accepted concepts in the positive psychology-emotional wellness literature known for promoting self-improvement and personal fulfillment. What I have done is collate them and attempt to bring them to life through the telling of stories involving everyday events.

Because that is where I believe you will find true and enduring happiness – within yourself in the everyday things that you do. Be it driving a car to work, playing with your children, trawling for bargains at a trash and treasure market, or watching honey bees do their thing in the front garden. Greater happiness, as the stories will show, can be yours at anytime you choose.

Then, at the end of each story, you have the option of discovering how to put each secret into practice using a smorgasbord of happiness activities in the second part of the book, Practice Happiness. Alternatively, you may prefer to kick back with the cat on your lap, a good brew at your fingertips, and continue reading the stories.

There is no right order for reading the stories or completing the activities. It's entirely up to you and your needs. My one hope is that you enjoy reading the stories and that they may provoke moments of self-discovery.

However, to get the most from the book and to make it as enjoyable an experience as possible let me offer you a few suggestions:

Read the stories first

You may like to simply read all the stories first to get a feel for the book and an overview of the happiness secrets. You could read the stories in sequence or you could pick and choose based upon titles that grab your interest.

Scribble some notes

If you're like me I love to jot down revelations or insights in the margins when I read books. Go for it. This is your happiness project. Make the most of the moment.

Focus on one story

You might choose to focus on one particular story. Mull over it for a while and roll it around your mind like a boiled sweet. What is the message? How is the message relevant for your life? (Assume that it is.) How could your life be improved by investing in the message? (Assume that it could be.) Get motivated.

Check out the activities

After reading a story you can explore the relevant activities in the second part of the book. Browse through them seeing what is involved. Continue building your motivation for a life makeover.

Practice the activities

Crunch time! Sooner or later you'll reach the moment where you have to decide to commit to completing some of the activities. How important is being happier to you? How important is your improved happiness for the people in your life? Remember that to change *your* level of happiness you have to make changes to *your* life.

Share what you learn with others

I strongly encourage you to discuss your discoveries with your partner, or your best friend, or your parents. As well as being fun and a source of happiness in itself, talking about it with someone else will help you clarify the concept in your mind and, hopefully, commit you to taking action.

Becoming happier requires you take action

I have friends who have read dozens upon dozens of self-help books but have not changed their lives one iota. Why? They read the stories, nod their heads, perhaps make some notes but then they choose not to do the most important thing – they don't complete any of the recommended activities or put any of the concepts into practice. So their lives stay the same. And in exasperation they tell me, "I read that book and it didn't help me one little bit." However when a person chooses to diligently apply the ideas they have read *just one book* can make all the difference to their life.

So, my thoughts and my best wishes are with you as you take this journey towards a happier and more fulfilled you. Know that having started down this path your life will never be the same. You deserve to be happy and you are taking steps to make it happen. Be proud of this fact. And look for signs of happiness around you every day and remember that the potential for happiness is always within you *anywhere anytime.*

PART ONE

The Happiness Secrets

Chapter

1

Live from the Inside Out

Be the person you are meant to be

1

Girlfriend at the Cinema

Your feelings of happiness are your own responsibility

"DON'T YOU WANT TO MAKE ME HAPPY?"

Putting an old girlfriend on the spot. Hitting her with *that* question. The one that causes flies to freeze in midflight and makes dogs whimper and crawl under divans. Emotional blackmail 101.

You see, I want to watch the latest Bond movie at the cinema. And she doesn't. She's all set to buy a ticket for *Pretty Woman*. I'm thinking, *"How can she not want to watch the Bond movie knowing how happy that would make me feel?"* Maybe that means she wants me to be unhappy. *(Keep in mind this is the logic of a 20-year old male.)* So I have a temper tantrum right there. And grumble under my breath about how unfair it is that someone else should be in charge of my happiness.

Sounds crazy I know but this type of thinking can creep into a relationship right under your nose. As the girlfriend and I spent more and more time together I stopped doing many of the things I had previously enjoyed doing as a single guy like hanging out with my best friends, going to the gym, and exploring weekend markets. I began neglecting my own happiness. Gradually I started absolving myself of more and more responsibility for my own feelings while placing the burden of responsibility for these feelings on her. Pretty soon I was holding her accountable for my happiness.

On the flipside, I started blaming her for some of my own unhappiness. If I felt bored I'd blame her for not keeping me entertained. And I'd blame her for making me feel frustrated when we had arguments over misunderstandings – I mean, she should know what I'm trying to say, shouldn't she? *(There's that logic again.)*

I was busy blaming other people for my feelings too. I'd blame bosses for making me miserable when they gave me extra work. I'd blame referees for making me cranky at football games. I'd blame slow drivers for making me so angry I'd strangle the steering wheel and yell like a crazed madman. Whenever I felt unhappy I'd find someone to blame.

And then one day my view of the world was turned upside down. I had my Eureka moment. Of the earth-isn't-flat magnitude. I'd convinced myself that my feelings were at the beck and call of others. But while working on my PhD in stress management I realized that I'd had everything back to front. Turns out you are responsible for your own emotions. And here's the reason – *your thoughts determine your feelings.* The way you think about things, the way you choose to interpret what happens to you, determines the feelings you have.

When your boss barks at you to enter his office during a corporate shake-up you might choose to feel excited, possibly anticipating a promotion, or you might feel anxious, worrying that you're about to be made redundant. Starting a new life with your beloved might make marriage exciting for you, while the prospect of giving up some independence might make it dispiriting for your spouse. The death of a family member can lead to a morbid fear of death or it might inspire you to do more with your life. Quite simply, regardless of the situation, whether you're stuck in traffic or have just been asked out on a date, how you interpret and react to a situation is your choice and *always your responsibility and no one else's.*

And so, time to man up. How should I have responded when the girlfriend told me she didn't want to watch the Bond film?

Well, I'll tell you how I respond today when my partner and I go to the movies. First of all, before a word slips from my mouth I remind myself that I am responsible for my own thoughts and emotions. Any feelings I have start and stop with me. Second, I resolve to respect her movie choice. Third, because I love her and have come to realize that a relationship is more about giving than receiving, I usually acquiesce to her choice. Fourth, if I am hell-bent on watching an action flick and feel that it would make me feel happy then….I GO AND WATCH AN ACTION MOVIE….by myself if I have to (*which she is happy with by the way*). I take ownership of my own feelings and do not rely on her for my happiness. And I know - because she tells me – a woman finds emotional independence in her man a whole lot more attractive than a man who is a clingy needy sour puss.

The point is that you can be happy – and should be happy – when you are single. Happiness comes from within. Then having developed the ability to generate your own feelings of happiness, when you enter into a relationship, you can hope to be *happier*.

Taking full responsibility for your own happiness and all of your feelings is the foundation stone of building a life of happiness. The key to a life of purpose and meaning, of fulfilling and loving relationships, and of being all that you can be, starts right here.

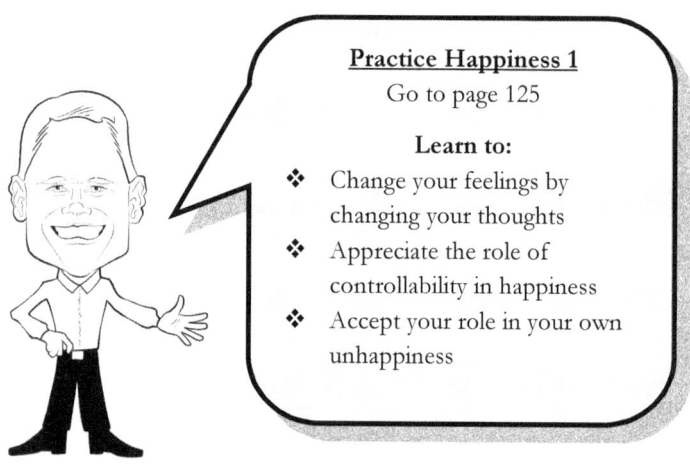

Practice Happiness 1
Go to page 125

Learn to:

❖ Change your feelings by changing your thoughts
❖ Appreciate the role of controllability in happiness
❖ Accept your role in your own unhappiness

2

Scouts

Be prepared to take responsibility for your circumstances

THE LOCAL SCOUT GROUP MEETS IN THE HALL down the end of the street. Every Wednesday night you can hear their raucous yells and stamping feet. They're reciting solemn oaths and discovering special handshakes. And learning how to pitch tents and build fires without matches. They're practicing using compasses and tying double fisherman's knots. And they're trying to earn a zillion merit badges.

They're getting prepared.

They're getting prepared to be able to handle whatever curved balls life throws at them. Because that's what the scout motto says — *Be Prepared*. But it's not meant to be confined to parade grounds and campsites. In truth, it's a motto for life.

Take Georgina Sutton for example. At 17 years of age she went gliding with a scout flying club in South Australia and fell in love with the feeling of flying over the countryside and soaring with eagles. Within two years she gained glider and power licenses through the club. The scouts had planted the seeds for her future dreams and ambitions. And she was ready for the challenge. *Be Prepared*.

She set her sights on becoming a pilot with Australia's national airline, Qantas, the "Flying Kangaroo." First, however, she had to gain a commercial pilot's license. Five years of hard work and sacrifice followed. She saw mistakes as necessary feedback and setbacks as tests of her resolve. She learnt to anticipate the unexpected. *Be Prepared.*

Then she needed flying experience and lots of it. So, the next five years were spent working with small airlines running scenic tours, flying charters and ferrying miners. Every job was a carefully considered stepping stone towards her ultimate goal. *Be Prepared.*

And then the day arrived when she got the call from Qantas. The young woman who had never travelled further abroad than New Zealand would now be piloting flights to Singapore and London.

But wait there's more. She worked as an airline pilot for 25 years, all the while improving her value within the company. She worked on her ability to handle flight deck problems, became a better team player, and contributed to the skill development of other pilots. And today, at 52 years of age, she has been rewarded for her efforts by becoming the first female fleet captain for Qantas, in charge of all the national airline's Boeing 767 planes and more than 180 pilots. (In a field where only 5% of all pilots are female.) *Be Prepared.*

A large measure of Georgina Sutton's success has been her eagerness to take ownership of whatever circumstances she finds herself in. This is straight out of the Scout Handbook. When things don't go as planned – being unable to light a fire, having a disagreement with a fellow scout, or leading a patrol down a wrong track – scouts are taught to confront the situation head-on as a challenge to be solved, not an excuse to hightail it, or an opportunity to look for someone to blame.

I mention this because our society seems to be in the midst of a blame game craze which is completely at odds with the scout creed. Have you heard any of these excuses lately?

"I got a parking fine. *How can they expect anyone to read that sign?*"
"I can't find my car keys. *Someone must have moved them.*"
"My partner left me. *Why do I keep meeting selfish men?*"
"I'm unhappy in my relationship. *My partner has become so boring.*"
"I keep missing out on promotions. *The boss obviously hates me.*"
"I got caught for speeding. *But everyone else was over the limit.*"

"My life sucks. I'm so miserable. *It was my lousy upbringing.*"

"Exercise? Are you kidding? *I don't have time to exercise.*"

As soon as you make excuses or blame someone else for your circumstances you disempower yourself. You relinquish control of part of your life. Your energy levels, your confidence and creativity, your dreams, your ability to soldier on are all put on hold. In order to be all that you can be you have to be prepared to take responsibility for dealing with whatever situation you find yourself in.

This is the very essence of the scout motto – *Be Prepared.*

Former scouts, like Georgina Sutton, live this motto every day by taking responsibility for their circumstances. They roll up their sleeves, put on their thinking caps, and get busy finding solutions. And so can you.

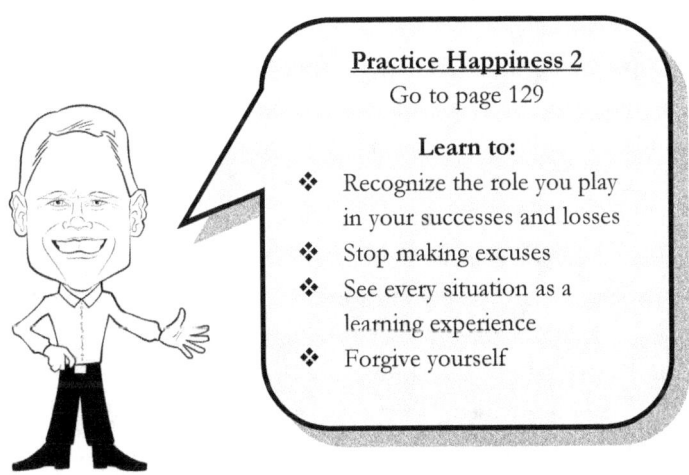

Practice Happiness 2
Go to page 129

Learn to:
❖ Recognize the role you play in your successes and losses
❖ Stop making excuses
❖ See every situation as a learning experience
❖ Forgive yourself

3

Reality TV Star

Recognize your strengths and ignite your passion

THIS STORY IS ABOUT A TRUE HERO. She's forty-seven years old, unmarried, is an unemployed charity worker, and is living alone with her cat in a small village in Scotland. Her one true pleasure is singing. Every chance she gets she sings in church choirs and at village pubs. Occasionally she participates in singing competitions. Singing is her passion. But what she wants, what she *really* wants is to be a professional singer. This has been her dream for as long as she can remember.

The year is 2009. And she is about to get her opportunity to sing in front of a large audience. A very large audience. Friends and family have persuaded her to audition for Britain's Got Talent, a reality TV talent show. With a live audience of several hundred and over ten million viewers she strides to the center of the stage hands on hips, portly, frumpily dressed, sporting a mat of grey frizzy hair. When asked by one of the judges how successful she would like to be she shoots back in a thick accent, "Elaine Paige or someone like that." Amidst titters and much head shaking from the audience she quietly composes herself, adopts a countenance of steely determination, lowers her brow....and begins to sing.

Astonishing. Spine-tingling. Uplifting. The audience and millions of others just like myself around the world were at first dumbstruck and then mesmerized by the sound that floated from her mouth. She may not have the honeyed looks of a Taylor Swift, the ethereal virtuosity of a Whitney Houston, nor the breakneck gyrating stage presence of a Beyonce, but she has a voice that would stop a host of angels in midflight. I am sure that by now you have figured out the name of my hero – Susan Boyle – and that four years on from singing "I Dreamed a Dream" from *Les Miserables* she has made millions, been on all the talk shows, met the Queen, and the rest. Most importantly, she is realizing her dream each and every day.

There are three key ingredients behind Boyle's success. First, she knew with her whole being that singing was her strength and that if she persisted, despite a lifetime of obstacles, she could succeed. All she needed was the opportunity to sing in front of a large audience. And eventually she got it. Her's was no overnight success. Overnight fame perhaps, but not overnight success. While waiting for her chance she had been honing her craft, in a range of environments, and in front of a variety of different people. Look at any individual who is outstanding at what they do, such as Olympians or concert musicians or neurosurgeons; they have all mastered their craft through years and years of practice, discipline, constant self-improvement, and self-belief.

You can recognize these kinds of people in your community in several ways – they are acknowledged for being excellent in their field, they are more focused and engaged when working, they experience less stress and are more resilient to setbacks, they are passionate about what they do, they are full of energy and vitality, they are more confident in themselves, and they are happier because they feel that they are fulfilling their potential which gives their life more meaning.

The second ingredient is her refusal to cow down to the prejudices and expectations of others. It is remarkable that, after forty-seven long years of being reminded day after day that she was the antithesis of what successful singers are meant to look like – she was neither young nor glamorous nor clad in a skimpy outfit – she still had sufficient reserves of courage and self-conviction to keep striving for her dream. Extraordinary. A Scottish Cinderella with the doggedness and self-belief of a Rocky Balboa.

And just how did she prevent the assumptions and beliefs of others from derailing her own dreams? She chose not to compare herself to others while remaining totally locked on to her own unique strength. People would judge her by her voice, not by her appearance.

The final ingredient behind Boyle's success was the hope that one day, provided she continued developing her singing talents and didn't buy into the conventional wisdoms of talent show success, her decision to focus all her energies into singing would pay off. This meant having to define the currency of her success. Susan Boyle dreamed of being a professional singer and performing to large audiences. In her eyes she was and is successful on both counts.

You have your own unique strengths. All you need is the courage to follow them. Even though the path is likely to be littered with obstacles, it is these very obstacles that will test and strengthen your commitment. And once you commit, *truly commit*, to developing your strengths you will ignite your passion and be on your way to achieving your own dreams.

Practice Happiness 3
Go to page 134

Learn to:
❖ Identify your strengths
❖ Make the greatest use of your strengths
❖ Avoid listening to others' expectations of you

4

Green Turtle

Trusting in your values will keep you on course

THE YEAR IS 1953. As a contented Edmund Hillary gazes out over the Himalayas from the summit of Mount Everest, 6,000 miles away on a small Pacific island a baby green turtle gazes warily up and down the beach before making a mad scramble to the sea. She's got a tough road ahead of her. Over the coming years she'll face voracious sharks, the whims of ocean currents, a measly menu of whatever floats past her table, and an ever-increasing number of plastic bags and fishing nets and oil spills. Her mission is to become a mother.

Fast forward to 2013. It's the middle of January, the height of the Australian summer, and I'm holidaying on the stunningly beautiful Heron Island on Australia's Great Barrier Reef. On a sand dune shrouded in darkness a wildlife ranger is telling a story about a female green turtle that has just returned to her birthplace to continue the cycle of life.

It's the *same* turtle. Do the math.

I crane forward to pay homage to this ancient mariner, this Magellan of the seas. She's the size of a tractor tire weighing over 200kg with an olive-streaked brown shell, a small rounded head, front flippers that form wide long wings and hind flippers that look like a baseball catcher's mitt. She's hard at work digging an egg chamber. You see, every five years she makes a 2000 mile-long voyage across open oceans to return to this island to lay her eggs. But not just any part of the island, mind you.

She returns to the *same beach*.

She is able to surf up on to the *same patch of sand* that she scampered down as a baby. She hits the bull's-eye every time. Her secret? A tiny magnetic lump in her brain which always points true north.

Turns out you have got your own personal compass. Not the heavy metal stuff that Sally has. Your compass is your set of personal values. They are the things you stand for and care about most. Things like wealth, security, health, honesty, and family. They are your foundation motivators that cause you to behave the way you do. On a compass your values represent true north. On your journey through life they represent your true self.

Whenever you are faced with tough decisions and are unsure which direction to take, stop and pull out your compass and consult your values. Should you buy that new Jeep when you have just started a new job? Should you stay in that relationship knowing that your boyfriend doesn't want children? Is now the right time to be getting a mortgage? Checking the prioritization of your values will allow you to answer these questions intelligently and with confidence.

For example, what do you do when you are offered a higher paying job with longer working hours knowing that it will compromise the time you can spend with your family? If success and wealth are amongst your top values, you will probably accept the job offer. If family and health are higher values, you will decline the offer. The best bit is that your feelings will confirm that you made the right decision.

Think of the compass again. Your values represent true north and your decision represents a compass bearing to your goal. When the two are aligned you are in harmony and will feel calm and satisfied and happy. You are living your values. You are being true to yourself.

But when you set compass bearings – that is, make decisions or behave in ways – that are not aligned with your values you experience disharmony which will lead to unpleasant feelings of frustration, confusion, indecision, emptiness or unhappiness.

Knowing your values and their relationship to your feelings puts you in the box seat for taking control of your life. You can now map out the future you want by aligning your everyday behaviors – your compass bearings – with your preferred values. And just keep readjusting your behaviors until you get the feelings you want. You need a challenging job to get you bouncing out of bed every morning? Then take a compass bearing and speak to your boss or change jobs. Having a partner who shares your love of the outdoors is important to you? Then take a compass bearing and join bushwalking clubs or cycling groups. Being fit and healthy is one of your top values? Then take a compass bearing and make it happen.

Your values represent a powerful avenue for influencing your behaviors and feelings. And, just like Sally and her onboard compass, when you listen to them faithfully they will always guide you to your true destination.

(By the way, Sally is expected to continue visiting the island till 2103.)

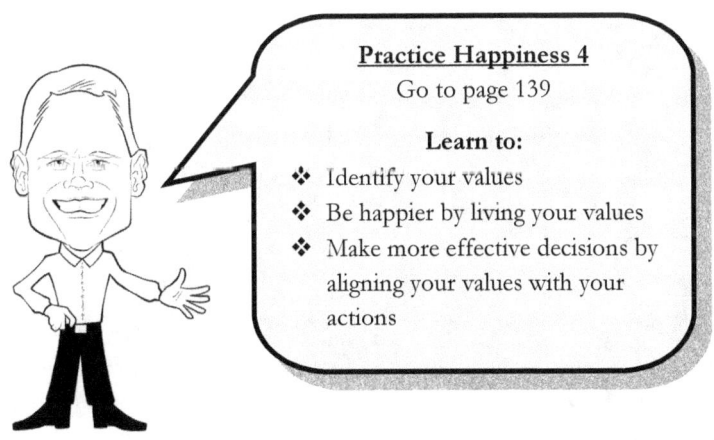

Practice Happiness 4
Go to page 139

Learn to:

❖ Identify your values
❖ Be happier by living your values
❖ Make more effective decisions by aligning your values with your actions

5

Climbing Trees

Don't let yourself be pigeon-holed

KIDS LOVE CLIMBING TREES. I think it's built into our DNA. As three-year olds we start off trying to shinny up the legs of dining room tables because up on top is where all the food seems to be. Then there are floor-to-ceiling bookcases to explore and kitchen cupboards to pillage. Later on we progress on to scaling backyard trees like weeping willows and oaks and figs, and we peer down on our neighbors from cubby houses perched in the upper branches of raggedy old conifers.

What's your most memorable tree climbing experience? What makes it so unforgettable? Was it the size of the tree? The friend who was beside you? The holiday house you were staying in? My favorite climb belongs to a 70 meter giant called the Gloucester Tree.

Nestled within the majestic karri forests of southern Western Australia, the Gloucester Tree was already a teenager when Captain Cook sailed into Botany Bay in 1770. Today it stands proudly as a giant among giants, honored as the highest fire lookout tree in the world. Maintaining a fixed upwards gaze you wind your way up, and up and up, a spiral staircase of 153 steel pegs that sprout from the tree's massive silvery-grey colored trunk. When at last you reach the top, slightly giddy and breathless, you are rewarded with a 360 degree unimpeded view of the surrounding forests. You feel like you're sitting atop Treebeard in Tolkien's Middle Earth. Jack at the top of the beanstalk.

Over the years I have assembled a small forest of bonsai, or miniature trees that mimic full-size trees, to remind me of some of my more exciting climbs. After successfully scaling the Gloucester Tree I felt that I had earned the right to add a karri bonsai to my modest collection.

However, the resident horticulturalist at my local nursery explained to me that some trees are not so easily tamed. While many tree varieties lend themselves to the Japanese art of bonsai some of the giant varieties do not. And the imperial karri is one of these. Despite repeated pruning of their branches and cutting back their roots they keep outgrowing their pots. They simply refuse to be contained. Nature has placed them on the earth for a reason and they must spread their roots far and wide to fulfill their purpose.

This makes me think that maybe some people are not meant to be potted either. You know the ones. Those people who refuse to play by the rules: the school graduate who decides to break with family tradition and become a vet instead of an engineer; the woman who elects to start her own business teaching unemployed youth work skills rather than settle for a high paying job she is qualified for but doesn't find satisfying; the thirty year old who risks all his savings to pursue a career as a writer instead of being chained to a mortgage; the middle-aged couple who sell up and move to Indonesia to do missionary work.

Every day people like this are making the choice to break free of the shackles of societal expectations and forge their own paths. Feeling like square pegs in round holes they realize that the well traveled road is not for them. They know that there is someone they are meant to be and that they will not become that person living a life governed by the rules and expectations of others. They know that allowing themselves to be pigeon-holed would rob them of the opportunity to be everything they could be.

The most commonly expressed regret by people on their death bed is, "I wish I'd had the courage to live a life true to myself, instead of the life others expected of me."

Be courageous. Refuse to be tamed. This is your time to shine.

And I hope children (and big people) keep climbing trees.

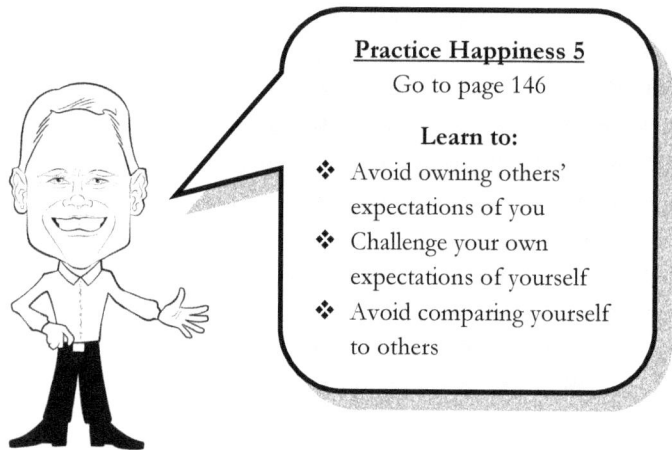

Practice Happiness 5
Go to page 146

Learn to:
❖ Avoid owning others'
   expectations of you
❖ Challenge your own
   expectations of yourself
❖ Avoid comparing yourself
   to others

6

Football Cheer Squad

Be your very own cheer squad

MY FAVORITE EXPERIENCE AS A KID was going to the football with my dad on a Saturday. We barracked for Carlton – the Old Dark Navy Blues – one of the oldest teams in the competition. Decked out in winter coats with scarves snaked around our necks and beanies pulled down tight over our ears we made the weekly pilgrimage, along with legions of other fans, to Princes Park, Carlton's home ground. Once we arrived, dad and I would thread our way through the milling crowd to our favored square meter of standing space close to the northern goal posts.

Barely ten meters away, directly behind the goal posts, was the hallowed domain of the Carlton cheer squad, a tribal group of fifty diehard supporters. Led by a mountainous John Candy lookalike, half the members wore duffle coats festooned with badges and flags and player portraits, the other half sported club jerseys which proudly displayed the numbers of their favorite players.

Prior to kickoff, the cheer squad held up 2-storey-tall crepe paper banners on the playing field, banners bearing slogans like "We're contenders, not pretenders" and "The mighty blues – always relentless" and "We believe in you 100% – you're absolute champions." The players, giants with tree-trunk legs and arms of steel, would then run through the banners to the thunderous applause of the crowd.

This was the 1970s and Carlton legends of the game included the shaggy-haired defender Bruce Doull, dubbed "the flying doormat", "Big Nick" John Nicholls, a ruckman who routinely flattened opponents who made the mistake of manhandling his teammates, and the aerial wizard Alex Jesaulenko, whose every leap into the air brought the crowd to its feet with an explosive roar of "JEZZZZAAAAA" that could be heard a full mile away.

The cheer squad's unflinching support of their heroes never waned throughout the game, irrespective of the score. When a player missed a shot at goal or was reprimanded by the umpire, calls of encouragement greeted his ears, while if the opposing team gained the upper hand, the club song was chanted and club flags of blue and white waved to and fro. When a player successfully eluded his opponent or displayed a flash of ball wizardry, the cheer squad punched their beach ball-sized pom poms into the air and hollered out "Carlton." And when their beloved team booted a goal, the supporters behind the goal posts simply ERUPTED. Fists pummeled the boundary fence, pom poms shot up and down like pistons, tentacle-like streamers frantically swished back and forth. You almost expected the roof of the grandstand to fly off at any moment. And then, at the end of the game, as their heroes with shoulders bowed and nursing bruised limbs limped from the ground, the cheer squad paid homage to their courage and tenacity with a final rousing rendition of the club song.

You know, I think it would be pretty cool having your very own cheer squad. A small team of cheerful and resolute personal trainers all wearing t-shirts emblazoned with your name and rallying cries like "Every day I am getting closer to my goal" and "It's not about how bad I want it, it's about how hard I am prepared to work for it." When you're ready to quit, they'd be imploring you to dig deep and push out two extra reps on the bench press and crunch ten more abs. They'd be right beside you with the boom box blaring out the Rocky anthem when you're pounding the pavement at six on drizzly winter mornings. When going for that job interview they'd be lining the walls offering encouraging nods and winks. When going on first dates they'd guarantee you remain upbeat and attentive to your companion. When at a restaurant they'd be helping you monitor your portion sizes and recall your goal weight. And when feeling down in the dumps or that the whole world is against you they'd be urging you to cut yourself some slack and practice a bit of self-compassion.

Having a personal cheer squad at your beck and call would definitely have its own advantages. But it would start to get a bit expensive and would probably be frowned upon by suitors and employers.

The alternative is to....*be your very own cheer squad.*

On hand 24/7, and totally answerable to you, your very own cheer squad will be entrusted with just one responsibility – keeping you positive. You'll design your own motivating environment and wallow in it every day. You'll limit your exposure to negativity from the media and from people who make you feel down. You'll be your own best friend and encourage yourself every step of the way towards your goals and you'll lift yourself up whenever you face setbacks or are feeling low. And you'll make it glaringly obvious to one and all that you – YOU – are your own cheer squad by the way you respect and look after yourself.

What are you waiting for? Start cheering today!

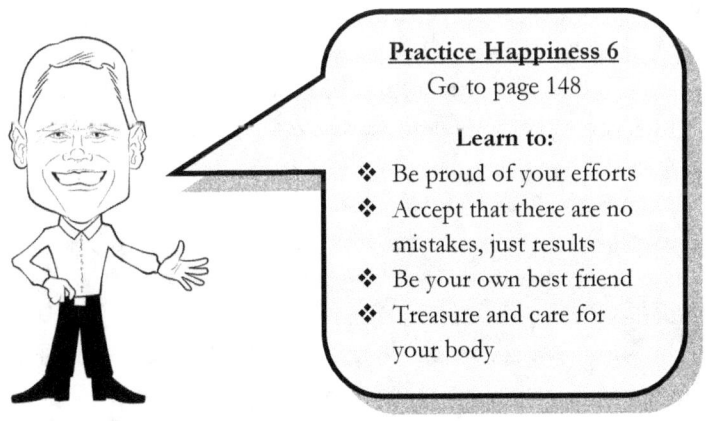

Practice Happiness 6
Go to page 148

Learn to:
❖ Be proud of your efforts
❖ Accept that there are no mistakes, just results
❖ Be your own best friend
❖ Treasure and care for your body

7

Stormtrooper

Find a cause greater than yourself

A LONG TIME AGO IN A NEIGHBORHOOD far, far away....

It was 1977 and Star Wars fever was at its peak. There was a disturbance in the Force as young Jedi Apprentices up and down the street were being seduced by the Dark Side.

At 18 Roderick Street, armed with dazzling hand gestures and a permanent scowl, I marched around the family home to the dum dum da-dum of the Imperial March trying to exploit the power of the Force. Yet no matter how often I waved my hand across my face saying, "I am NOT the volunteer you are looking for", I still got roped into washing the dishes. And the lock on the kitchen pantry remained firmly locked. Heck, I couldn't even convince my cocker spaniel to bite my sisters. Anyway, word must have gotten out because I was promptly dumped from Darth Vader's team of future disciples.

Fortunately, Obi-Wan and Yoda must have been looking out for me. Because it was around this time that I was involved in a snowball drive collecting donations to help feed disadvantaged kids. It was a momentous experience. Like being zapped by a lightsaber. It freed me from the evil clutches of the Dark Side. And revealed the secret to harnessing the Force – giving service freely to others.

But there's more to this story. If you think Stars Wars characters only exist on the big screen, then think again. Because years later the unthinkable happened.

I met a *real live* stormtrooper.

It was a Monday morning, January, 2012. I'm driving through the streets of Adelaide when I pass a stormtrooper on the side of the road. *A fully decked out Imperial stormtrooper* – complete with battle armor and helmet. I kid you not. After scanning the sky for a hovering Star Destroyer I park the car and jog over to him.

The stormtrooper's name is Jacob French. A 21 year old sales assistant from Western Australia. He is half-way through a nine month walk across the country from Perth to Sydney. He tells me that he has just notched up 1700 miles, nine tenths of them across the Nullarbor Plain, a flat treeless wasteland of searing day temperatures, freezing cold nights, snakes, and relentless biting insects. The whole time wearing his white armor and pushing a 50kg buggy containing a simple stormtrooper's worldly belongings. He has walked over ten hours each day – about 45 km – before settling down to an evening of blister inspections and instant noodles.

The more I listen to his story the more I wonder if he is serving a punishment for a stormtrooper conduct violation (like hitting his head on a control room doorway in a Death Star – *a scene from the Star Wars movie*). But I couldn't be more wrong. French has taken the year off hoping to march the 3106 miles across the continent to raise funds for the Starlight Children's Foundation, a charity that helps sick children in need.

And, if you're wondering, yes, he does make it. He strides into the Sydney Children's Hospital 268 days after beginning his odyssey. In all he raises over $98,500.

The force was strong with that one. He may have been dressed as a stormtrooper but a Jedi Knight, he surely was.

Every day ordinary people just like Jacob French are becoming Jedi Knights by performing extraordinary acts of selflessness and generosity for charity groups and community organizations. Some are knocking on doors for fundraisers. Some are acting as reading mentors for children of poor families. Some are serving meals at homeless shelters. Others are providing entertainment to cancer victims in hospitals or delivering Christmas gifts to needy children. And others still are marching across the country in fancy dress costumes. All of these people who voluntarily give up their time and energy and skills have found a cause greater than themselves – helping and being of service to others.

Following this path provides its own rewards. Not only is your heart filled with more compassion and love for your neighbor, but you become happier and more at peace and less troubled by daily stressors.

It was Mahatma Gandhi who said, *"The best way to find yourself is to lose yourself in the service of others."*

Now there was a guy who knew a thing or two about the Force.

Practice Happiness 7
Go to page 153

Learn to:
❖ Discover a charitable cause that interests you
❖ See all the benefits you will gain from committing to your cause
❖ Commit to your cause

8

Investment Banker

Live a life of meaning and enjoy a meaningful life

HAVING A DEEP-AND-MEANINGFUL was the cool thing to do when you were a university student back in the 80s. No membership required, no pony tails necessary, just a willingness to listen to the psychedelic music of Pink Floyd and toss back flaming shots of Galliano.

Sessions typically began with the more humdrum questions like "Does pressing the elevator button repeatedly make it come sooner?" and "Where do birds go to die?" Then, once the lubricants had worked their magic and lightning bolts of wisdom were ricocheting around the circle, the heavy duty questions were tackled. Brain busters like "Why are you, you?" and "If the average human life span was 40 years, how would you live your life differently?" And then the granddaddy of all questions, "What is the meaning of life?"

Twenty-five years later on and the meaning of life continues to leave students flummoxed and tongue-tied. And they're not the only ones. It's the hottest topic at most of the dinner parties I attend nowadays. We're all at that midlife point where we've worked hard to get the steady job, the family with 1.5 kids, the house with the backyard, the annual holiday to Bali and we're beginning to wonder - just a little nervously – if this is as good as it gets. What does it all mean? Am I fulfilling my purpose? Just WHAT IS my purpose?

Then along comes Andrew. Late-thirties, average height with neat blonde hair, self-assured, carefree. We were introduced at a friend's barbecue. Let me share his story with you.

Ten years previously he was living the Generation Y dream. Investment banking whiz earning a six-digit salary, owner of two properties, a BMW M3 in the garage, Armani suits and handmade Berluti shoes – all the trappings of success. His entire focus was about making money and his favorite pastime was finding ways to spend money. Every time he closed a deal, gained a promotion, or bought another gadget he felt happy and satisfied.

And for a time this fulfilled him. But then he started noticing that his feelings of fulfillment were being replaced by feelings of extreme emptiness. His crossroad moment came when in one week his girlfriend walked out on him and his brother told him that he had become a self-obsessed materialistic-driven jerk. Ouch!

To his great credit he used the moment to reflect upon the meaning of his life. And he wasn't very happy with what he found. So – *here comes my favorite part of the story* – so the next week he resigned from his job and went hitch-hiking around Asia!

Most of the time he spent in the Philippines staying with local families, sometimes in the wealthier areas and sometimes in the poorer neighborhoods. Noticing the obvious disparities between the rich and the poor he was struck by the fact that both groups seemed to be about as happy as each other. This got him thinking about the balance of satisfying our needs versus being ruled by our wants. While wrestling with this problem serendipity stepped in when he was given the opportunity to participate in an international volunteer project. Another crossroads moment.

Upon returning to Australia he adopted a more modest lifestyle based on satisfying his needs. He enrolled in a community development degree, and began doing volunteer work with a couple of non-government humanitarian relief groups. For the past five years he has been employed with an international humanitarian aid organization as a program funding director, a position that uniquely allows him to use his strengths in finance to drum up much needed sponsors and benefactors. He says that he has never felt so fulfilled and passionate about his work because he is contributing to a worthwhile cause that is aligned with his highest value of service to others.

And his answer to the big question about the meaning of life? He rephrases the question to "What is the meaning of MY life?" He thinks that there is no one universal definition for everyone. Rather, it is up to each of us to bring meaning to our own lives. How we *choose* to do that – now THAT, is the real question.

I'm captivated by Andrew's story. And the idea that we bring meaning to our lives by having a sense of purpose in the way we live each day. And that we derive our sense of purpose by examining our strengths and passions, our values, and our belief in causes greater than ourselves.

Ultimately, it is our sense of purpose that we will be remembered for. This is our gift to the world. And the world needs what each of us has to offer.

So, what gift do you wish to give?

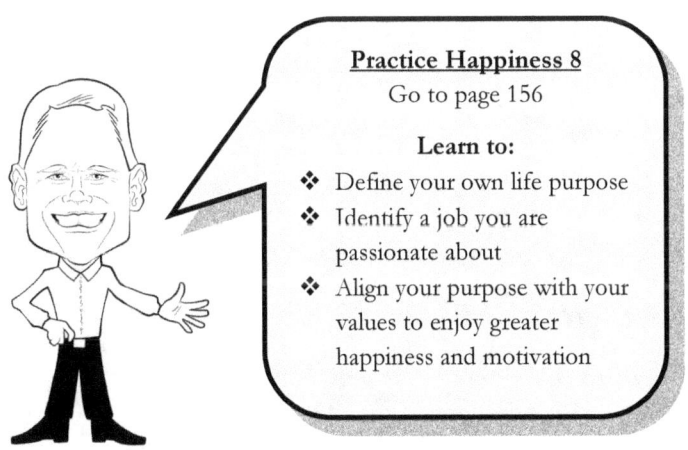

Practice Happiness 8
Go to page 156

Learn to:
❖ Define your own life purpose
❖ Identify a job you are passionate about
❖ Align your purpose with your values to enjoy greater happiness and motivation

Chapter

2

Live with a Positive Attitude

See the world with a sunny
confident outlook

9

Christmas

Your beliefs influence your feelings

"ENJOY THE BROWNIES AND HAVE A BLESSED MERRY Christmas."

"I will," I replied. "Thanks again, and a Merry Christmas to you both."

Exchanging season's greetings with the lovely middle-aged Christian couple from across the street who stopped by with some homemade fruit mince brownies and a psalm-inscribed bookmark. If you were to run a nation-wide search for a family embodying the whole Christmas travesty then you need not look any further.

Their single-storey bungalow home is straight out of *National Lampoon* covered in a spider web of multicolored bulbs and twinkling lights. The front yard a fairyland of trumpeting angels, carrot-nosed snowmen, life-size wooden nutcrackers, and solemn nativity scenes. Every night there's a carnival atmosphere as the Christian couple and their two children sing carols and distribute sweets to passers-by.

Then on Christmas morning they're off to church for fellowship and prayer before returning home to an afternoon of kinship when their driveway becomes a turnstile of visiting uncles and aunts and grandparents. And they're not above dabbling in a spot of holiday commercialism either. The Jet Ski they bought last year has yet to be baptized and every year Santa upgrades the kids' pushbikes.

Somehow they seem to be able to embrace all the conflicting meanings of Christmas and stay cheerful and happy. I envy them.

But it's not me – I'm a Christmas cynic. Every year I flounder in a whirlpool of emotions brought on by contradictory beliefs. I have trouble reconciling the rampant consumerism with celebrating the birthday of the baby Jesus. I'm disillusioned by the move to rechristen the greeting *Merry Christmas* to *Happy Holidays* and I wonder why Christmas cheer has to be manufactured in the first place. At times I feel a bit teary when I think about absent family and friends. And with the passing of each year I find myself pining for Christmas past. Of snuggling up to my parents on the sofa to watch *Miracle on 34th Street*. Of the annual trip into the city to gawk in wonder at the animated fairy tale characters that came to life in the windows of the Myer department store.

While Christmas Day may be a holiday for all it means something different for everybody. Some believe Christmas is all about gathering the whole clan together while others believe an intimate family affair is enough. Some believe that simple presents are sufficient while others feel a need to buy lavish gifts. And some believe that the birth of Jesus must be actively celebrated whereas others prefer celebrating extended shopping hours. Regardless of how people spend Christmas everyone wants to be happy. When we spend Christmas Day in a way that aligns with our beliefs about Christmas we can expect to be happy. On the other hand, when we spend it in a way that is at odds with our beliefs then it's likely we won't be happy.

Beliefs are like that. They can be empowering beliefs which work for us and produce pleasant feelings or they can be limiting beliefs which work against us and produce unpleasant feelings. Some people feel anxious once they reach their mid to late forties, the famed midlife crisis. They believe that their age and health are against them and that they are running out of time to achieve many of their life goals. In contrast, other mid-lifers are looking after their health and are excited by the endless opportunities available to them because of their life experience and extensive networks. Consider a woman who feels demoralized after failing to receive a positive response on an e-dating site. She believes it is further proof that she is undeserving of a loving relationship. Another woman is unaffected as she believes that the gentleman is simply looking for other qualities in a partner. Or how about a man who feels satisfied losing 4kg after a month's gym membership because he believes he fulfilled his expectations. Alternatively, another man may be despondent believing that losing any amount less than 6kg represents failure. The point is that we are the architect of our own beliefs. They are not fixed. We can change them at anytime. And by choosing empowering beliefs that support us and our goals we set ourselves on the path to having pleasant feelings.

Understanding this allows me to resolve my own mixed emotions about Christmas. Although a cynic I know that I am still responsible for my feelings over the festive season. And I want to be happy. I choose to be happy. So what do I believe in that is untainted by the hypnotic pull of commercialism? What do I believe in without reservation?

I am spellbound by a day when we all smile a bit easier, make more eye contact, and are kinder to each other. Beneath the madness of tinsel and wrapping paper the gifts of compassion and goodwill are free to give and always in need. These are the gifts I can believe in. So every year I take myself off to the Salvation Army to serve lunches to adults and deliver presents to underprivileged children. And this makes me happy.

Peace and goodwill, with a sprinkling of fairy dust, to all mankind.

<u>Practice Happiness 9</u>
Go to page 163

Learn to:

❖ Identify the limiting beliefs holding you back
❖ Challenge your limiting beliefs
❖ Replace your limiting beliefs with empowering beliefs that increase your confidence

10

Moon Landing

Free your mind of handbrake thoughts that hold you back

IT WAS THE HEIGHT OF THE SPACE RACE. The Soviets had just launched the first man into space and the Americans were kicking themselves that they were coming second in a two-horse race. In response, on May 25, 1961, President John F. Kennedy made his famous speech about man going to the moon.

"My fellow Americans. Unfortunately we won't be going to the moon. I may have spoken in haste earlier. We would *like* to go to the moon in this decade and do the other things, but we have to be realistic. So we will have to make do with doing the other things. Man has not gone to the moon yet for a very good reason – it can't be done. Well, not at the moment anyhow. Let me explain some of the reasons why we decided to abort the project. First, it would cost a prohibitive $25 billion to fund the Apollo program. Second, we don't have the technology to build a lunar module that could safely land on the moon. Third, the metal alloys needed to withstand the extraordinary high temperatures of atmospheric re-entry do not exist. Fourth, the integrated computer circuitry required for guiding the modules hasn't been invented yet. And finally, to be brutally frank, trying to land a manned spacecraft on a moving target hurtling through space a quarter of a million miles away and then return it safely to earth is a bit like trying to fire an arrow blindfolded at a moving target positioned behind a tree. Not easy at the best of times. But nevertheless, rest assured that if it can be done, if someone works out how to do it, then we, yes we, will *definitely* be the first to put a man on the moon. I make this solemn pledge to my fellow Americans. Thank you and God Bless America."

Of course, these were not the momentous words that the President uttered that day. In the speech he delivered he committed the entire resources of the country to a specific goal by a specific deadline and he broadcast it to the entire world – the United States would land a man on the moon and safely return him to earth before the end of the 1960s. Talk about putting your reputation and integrity on the line. Supreme folly or an act of stunning audacity? Well, you and I both know what transpired.

On Monday, 21 July, 1969, schoolchildren across Australia were sent home early to witness an extraordinary life-changing event. At 12:56pm on a cloudy day in the city of Melbourne, I along with my three sisters and mother, were all hunched around our black and white television set. We watched spellbound as Neil Armstrong planted his left foot tentatively on the powdery surface of the moon. And with that small step suddenly anything was possible.

ANYTHING.

The world instantly became a limitless sea of opportunities. Man showed that when he is utterly and completely 100 percent committed to a task the wheels of providence begin to turn and with each revolution the vibrations of destiny echo throughout the universe seeking out favorable circumstances turning dreams into reality.

We see these forces at work every day. When a baby bounces back on his feet after stumbling, when a child learning to ride a bike immediately jumps back on after falling off, when a girl refuses to be content with a grade of B+ in math and resolves to improve her grade, when a university graduate succeeds in gaining employment after repeated knockbacks, when every four years Olympians continue to break "unbreakable" records, when scientists make radical breakthroughs further contributing to the health and wellbeing of the community, and when ordinary mums and dads get out of bed every morning committed to their families' care.

In all these cases people refused to think the handbrake thought "I can't." Instead they told themselves "I can" and "I will". And they did. When you choose to say these words and you commit to them with your entire being certain things begin happening to help you realize your goal – circumstances become more favorable, important contacts are passed your way, you become more solution-oriented rather than problem-focused, you notice more opportunities, and your self-confidence improves as you assume greater control over your future.

Thomas Edison said, "If we did all the things we are capable of doing we would literally astound ourselves." The only thing holding us back is our own handbrake thoughts.

Imagine what you could achieve if you released your handbrake thoughts and committed every fiber of your being to your goal. All your strengths, all your energy, all your passion. An unstoppable juggernaut.

Just imagine.

Practice Happiness 10
Go to page 167

Learn to:
❖ Identify your handbrake thoughts
❖ Replace your handbrake thoughts with springboard thoughts that empower you

11

Public Service Health Announcement

Inoculate yourself against secondhand stress

THIS IS A PUBLIC SERVICE HEALTH ANNOUNCEMENT. The public are advised to remain on guard against the Secondhand Stress Virus (SSV).

SSV is a particularly contagious empathy-borne illness transmitted by sensitivity to other people's emotions. Coming into contact with people who are severely stressed may result in infection. The greater the carrier's stress and the greater a victim's sensitivity, the greater the likelihood of infection.

Once infected by another person's stress, SSV can cause high blood pressure, impaired digestion, insomnia, depression, fatigue, muscle tension, and poor memory. With a short incubation period of only 1 second it can quickly drain a victim's energy, cause feelings of confusion and anger and helplessness, and can make a person hyper-attuned to their own problems.

The principle reason SSV is so debilitating lies in its low controllability. Typically, a person is responsible for their own feelings of stress which can be controlled by altering one's thoughts and behaviors. Not so with SSV, because the stress is coming from another person which the victim is powerless to change. Worst of all is the tendency for infected victims to pass on their secondhand stress to others, thus continuing the cycle.

While anybody can catch this virus certain high risk groups have been identified. These include: those who come into contact with teachers, particularly around report submission time; secretaries of CEOs; bartenders and hairdressers; parents in charge of young children at supermarkets; people who willingly become emotional garbage dumps for others; all women (as opposed to men who are less in touch with their feelings); friends of chronic complainers, criticizers or drama queens; non-stop gossipers; and everybody at tax time.

The public should be alert for the onset of symptoms. The initial symptoms, although relatively innocuous, may indicate a predisposition towards empathy-related behavior. Watch out for people who yawn after they see others yawn *(If you just yawned consider seeing a specialist immediately.)* Watch for people who tend to sway from side to side on the couch when watching skiing events on TV. And watch for those who bawl uncontrollably during the closing scenes of films like *Bridges of Madison County* and *Titanic*.

Once a person is infected this insidious virus can lead to the appearance of much more troubling symptoms. Check if any of these apply to you:

You find yourself being drained of energy when watching meaningless stories on the TV news about the daily routines of celebrities, misplaced aliens, and police car chases.

You find yourself sticking pins into voodoo dolls while listening to your friends describing their break-ups.

You find yourself mirroring the frazzled-looking employee who rushes around the office like a multitasking tornado. Or you feel panic-stricken after listening to your boss's rants about her deadlines.

You find yourself having running battles with the kids after your stressed husband walks through the front door at night.

You find yourself clicking your pen in tense conference rooms and swinging your foot in dull waiting rooms when others are doing the same.

You find that the urge to hit your car horn in a traffic jam when others all around you are blasting theirs is simply irresistible.

At the moment no vaccine or preventive drug for immunity against SSV exists. However, it is easily treatable. There are several forms of treatment. The first set of recommendations is appropriate if you are an especially compassionate soul who chooses to listen to the gripes and grumbles of others. At this time it is advisable you set boundaries concerning the assistance you are prepared to offer and try and inject positivity into the conversation. Be assertive and remember that your own emotions take priority over another person's emotions. Bear in mind, if you sense that you are a magnet for anxious individuals, you should reflect on the following questions: Are you doing something to encourage these types of people to come to you? Is their attention somehow fulfilling your own needs?

Second, consider distancing yourself from sources of negativity such as depressing news broadcasts and whining colleagues. Not only will this recommendation allow you to escape infection but it will guarantee that you can't pass the virus on to others. This remedy involves focusing on the one thing within your control – your own reaction to the stressful person or situation. While you can't stop other motorists from hitting their car horns or your boss having an office meltdown, you can take responsibility for your own thoughts and feelings about these things.

And finally, to strengthen your own resistance to the stress around you it is important to maintain a diet of positivity in your life. Choose friends who are optimistic and cheery types, care for your physical wellbeing with regular exercise and a healthy food plan, and practice the skills of happiness.

END OF PUBLIC SERVICE HEALTH ANNOUNCEMENT.

<u>Practice Happiness 11</u>
Go to page 171

Learn to:

❖ Identify the origin of your own stress

❖ Manage your own stress

❖ See if you are a magnet for others who are stressed

❖ Avoid taking on the stress of others

12

My Father

Don't let your expectations control your happiness

MY FATHER TAUGHT ME MANY THINGS during my childhood. He taught me how to kick a football. He taught me about versatility and how a Swiss Army knife could be used for everything from tightening bicycle spokes to scaling fish. He taught me the value of patience when assembling Airfix models. He taught me how teamwork could solve even the hardest problems, including packing the car for a family holiday. And he taught me the value of perseverance when chasing goals, and to listen to my mother if I knew what was good for me.

Some of the most important lessons he taught me were about happiness.

One day we went to the Melbourne Zoo to check out fruit bats. (I was a huge Batman fan at the time). Clumps of large bats were hanging upside down and peering at us from defoliated branches, their black wings wrapped around their furry bodies.

A weird thought suddenly occurred to me, "Dad, how do they go to the toilet when they're hanging upside down like that?"

"Keep watching and you'll find out," he replied.

The bats must have been listening because the very next moment one complied by quickly flipping its body right side up, pooping, and then swinging back to its normal upside down position. This instantly caused a furor amongst the lower bats who squeaked and wobbled their wings in protest.

"Unreal!" I exclaimed. "Gee, I'd be angry if someone pooped on me. Not very fair, is it?"

"Fairness has nothing to do with it," said my father. "Those bats were just in the wrong spot at the wrong time, that's all. Next time they may think more carefully about where they roost. And I doubt if they're going to be angry for long – animals don't stew over things like we do, they just get on with it."

My father's words must have struck a chord because they came flooding back when we returned to the car to discover a parking ticket slapped on the windshield. Dad looked at the ticket, looked at the nearby traffic sign, and looked at his watch. We had overstayed our parking time by a measly 5 minutes. We exchanged glances.

"Fairness has nothing to do with it," I shrugged.

"Dead right," he replied. "It's our fault. We were in the wrong spot at the wrong time. We won't let it ruin our day." We both laughed and then went for ice creams.

My father had a wonderful ability of explaining things in terms that I could understand. And no matter what drama occurred in my life or anyone else's life, like a magician pulling a rabbit out of a hat he was always able to conjure a silver lining. Through his example I learned that feeling happy was up to me and that I could have these feelings at anytime I wanted. I didn't have to postpone feeling happy until I reached goals or fulfilled certain expectations.

When I was disappointed that I had not won all of my swimming races he preferred to comment on my improving race times, rather than dwell on my obsession with placings. He told me I should be happy.

When I complained that not all of my teammates had voted for me being the captain of the soccer team he explained that it isn't possible to please everyone and that I should be happy knowing that I always give my best to the team.

When I entered my 20s and expressed my frustration at not having a girlfriend I could do heaps of things with, he suggested I do those things anyway and just be happy.

Years later when I grumbled that I was still penniless and still studying at the age of thirty while most of my friends were well established in their careers and owned their homes, he remarked that everyone is different with their own unique needs and strengths. He said I should be happy with the road I was following.

And then days later when we spoke at the airport – following a family reunion to celebrate his 75th birthday – he kissed me on the cheek, looked me in the eye and said, "I love you Bruce. You make me very happy." I squeezed his hands and replied, "I love you too Dad. I'll talk to you soon."

He died unexpectedly a week later.

A legacy that my father left me was the gift of unconditional happiness. Being happy in the present, with no strings attached. Life is far too short and too fragile to be holding our happiness to ransom by constantly saying, "I'll be happy when...." It took me a long time to learn the lesson. I'm still learning the lesson today.

And that's okay. I try and honor my father's legacy every single day. Not by waiting till the house is paid off or the kids leave home, till I lose a certain amount of weight or till summer rolls around, but by allowing myself to be happy at anytime, in any place, for any reason.

I'm feeling pretty happy right now.

<u>Practice Happiness 12</u>
Go to page 175

Learn to:
- ❖ Realize the futility of thinking "I'll be happy when…."
- ❖ Realize that fairness is entirely your own interpretation
- ❖ Focus on your progress instead of solely on your outcomes

13

Cyclone

Look for a silver lining in every cloud

A SILVER LINING CAN EVEN BE FOUND in a cyclone. I know because the good people of Cairns in the far north of Australia showed me.

You'll find the town of Cairns nicely nestled between a heavily-forested mountain range and the sparkling azure waters of the Coral Sea. It's a wonderful hop-off point for four-wheel drive adventures into the rainforests and boat trips out to the Great Barrier Reef. On its northern and southern doorsteps sit two mighty rivers, the Mulgrave and the Barron, with most of the surrounding area being a flood plain. There are only two seasons here the dry and the wet. The dry is mainly dry, while the wet is wet. VERY WET. Forget cats and dogs raining down. Think pigs and cows instead. We're talking tropical monsoon country – cyclone country.

It was a Sunday. All day people had been calmly preparing for the arrival of Cyclone Steve, a modest category 2 cyclone packing winds of 90 miles per hour. Boats were moored in an orderly fashion, sandbags positioned around homes, car fuel tanks topped up, household provisions stockpiled. Locals were used to this routine. Cairns welcomes up to 4 cyclones each year.

I wasn't used to it. This was my first wet season and I was on the verge of pooping bricks. I spent most of the day anxiously listening to radio updates and watching the languorous wave of palm fronds outside my flat. At half past six, 30 minutes before Steve's expected arrival, I upended my mattress against my bedroom window and made a beeline for my foxhole beneath a table in the corner of the lounge room. There, cradling a battery-operated radio, first aid kit, water bottle, and my teddy bear Beethoven, I waited.

7pm. On the dot. WOOOSSSHHHH!! CRRUUNCH!! GGGRRSSHHH!! The noise was terrrrificcc. Imagine your home being passed back and forth through a gigantic car washing machine. Add to that a locomotive doing donuts up and down your street. And add to that the sound of your windows being sandblasted with foliage from the adjacent botanic gardens. And top it all off with a herd of cows tap dancing with gay abandon on your roof. After 20 minutes, as suddenly as it began....it stopped. The eye.

KNOCK KNOCK. I sit bolt upright. Who would be at my door in the middle of a cyclone? I crawl to the door and slowly turn the handle fully expecting to see the Grim Reaper.

"Bruce, how are you?" Two friends of mine from down the street waving bottles of beer. Long time residents of Cairns. "Got any candles?"

"Are you two mad?" I ask as I rustle up some candles. "The cyclone isn't over yet."

"No probs. We just want to check you're alright. Half-time's always a good ten to fifteen minutes long."

We sat and drank our beers and chatted and laughed and then they left. Locals. Amazing.

Over the next week I witnessed this happy-go-lucky attitude and sense of camaraderie again and again. Following the cyclone Cairns' residents were without power and water for four days. FOUR DAYS. The rivers either side of the town burst their banks flooding the highways cutting off Cairns from the outside world. Some of the streets resembled scenes from a post-apocalyptic film with razed trees, uplifted roofs, and fallen power lines. People had good reason to feel down on their luck and wallow in self-pity.

And their response?

They made the best of it. In small communities everywhere people organized themselves into small groups and they got busy helping each other. Yards were cleared of branches with chainsaws and lopping shears, broken windows were covered with sheets of plastic, and streams of thick mud were mopped up.

And there was fun to be had too. After cyclones, torrential rains displace much of the local wildlife leading to some unusual encounters. Crocodiles were spotted wandering the town centre while several cows surfed a distance of 17 miles to nearby Green Island. Many animals seek temporary refuge in people's homes too. I woke up one night to find a 4-meter long scrub python relaxing in my lounge and for weeks afterwards green tree frogs would nervously peer up at me from the toilet bowl.

For four days almost every street put on a barbecue with loaves of bread and sausages. And everyone was welcome. There was lots of consoling, lots of encouragement, and lots and lots of laughter. In the face of hardship locals look out for one another and, together with an indomitable sense of humor and levity, a strong resilient community spirit is forged. The locals are masters at finding a silver lining.

The people of Cairns taught me that no event, not even a cyclone, is good or bad. It is *our interpretation* that determines whether it is good or bad in our eyes. Regardless of whether the event was caused by us or not, we always have a choice about how we respond. We can stamp our feet and play the powerless victim role and scream "Why me?" or we can say to ourselves "How can I benefit from this experience?"

Benefits come in different forms. The residents of Cairns benefit from cyclones by developing greater resiliency, both individually and as a community.

So how could you benefit from problems in your own life? Being passed over for a promotion might signal a need to reassess your qualifications and leadership skills. Being involved in a car crash could be an opportunity to learn better defensive driving skills or practice more compassion. Missing the bus to work gives you a chance to meet new friends and enjoy a moment of stillness. Getting a stomach ulcer (happened to me) might be a signal that you need to re-examine your lifestyle. Repeated relationship break-ups might suggest that you would benefit from some counseling to explore your values and improving your ability to express your emotions.

For every situation there is a potential benefit, a worthwhile lesson, or a silver lining, if you choose to look for it.

Practice Happiness 13
Go to page 179

Learn to:
❖ See that how you choose to interpret a situation determines your emotions
❖ See that all situations, regardless of their scale or circumstances, are neither good nor bad
❖ Look for the benefit in any situation

14

Travel Packing

Wherever you go, there you are

HAVING A MEMORABLE TRIP IS ALL ABOUT PACKING the right stuff. I do a lot of travelling and I've learned a few things.

I've learned that no traveler ever envies how much luggage his neighbor has. Downsizing and streamlining are what it's all about. Once upon a time I was the weighted down pack mule dragging giant suitcases around airports. Not anymore. Now I get everything into a single carry-on daypack. I wear a coat that can be worn inside out, use multifunctional gadgets, wear drip-dry shirts and convertible pants, and carry miniaturized toiletries. I've got the bag packing down pat.

It's the other thing we have to pack when travelling that requires the most thought. The thing that many of us overlook. The thing that determines how much we enjoy our trip and how unforgettable our memories – *our state of mind*. The way we think about things and the way we look at things HERE are going to color all our experiences THERE so we want to make sure we're packing the right attitudes.

Several years ago I spent a month tripping around China. Believe me when I tell you that this is one very unique country. To fully appreciate its culture and customs you want to have the right attitudes squirreled away in your fanny pack. Let me give you a taste of some of the more noticeable conventions.

At meals, as the honored foreigner, you'll be constantly toasted with baijiu, a white wine that doubles as rocket fuel. So have your transport home prearranged. While all roads have marked lanes and traffic lights, realize that most locals consider their usage as optional. And you'll discover a fascination with covering everything in plastic from TV remotes to car seats. Being open to these differences is what makes travelling so exhilarating.

In China you need to be open-minded and set aside any judgments you may have about how people should live. There is fierce competition for relatively few university spots so expect to see young children going to school on weekends. The locals have no qualms about eating anything that crawls, scampers or trots, so neither should you. Be adventurous and dig in. And be prepared to hurl yourself into the rugby scrum queues in banks and at elevators, where as a foreigner, you'll probably be pushed to the front anyway.

Be prepared to ad-lib, to be flexible when confronted with unforeseen challenges. If the bus breaks down accept an offer to ride in a horse and cart. If you can't find any hair conditioner (and you won't) make do with shampoo. Each bump in the road is a chance for you to discover something new about yourself and to learn to stop sweating the small stuff. Expect mishaps and minor disasters. And if they happen accept them as rich cultural experiences. I had a few: rushing to a clinic with a stomach ulcer; having to take a week-long train trip to Tibet after a plane flight was cancelled; losing my phone in Shanghai. Each occasion extended my personal comfort zone and forced me to interact with more people.

In China you'll be swamped with opportunities to mix with the locals. Every person you come across, whether it is a market vendor or a tour guide, will see you as their personal English teacher and will hurry over for a chat. In turn, you'll be expected to show off some of your well-rehearsed Chinese phrases. Be curious, be audacious. Attack food with chopsticks, get lost in a river of bicycles, give a Tai Chi exercise class in the park a whirl, try some dumplings at one of the sidewalk eateries.

A small company I did some contract work for recently returned from a tour group holiday in China. Many of the group, particularly those individuals who were less judgmental and more resilient, were thrilled at experiencing a culture that contrasts so completely with western society. They felt like children in a candy shop with new surprises around every corner. However, others in the group only had complaints to share: the overly relaxed Chinese approach to time; the apparent lack of order on the roads; the greed of some shopkeepers. I noticed that the chronic nitpickers were the same people who were constantly finding fault with life before the trip.

All these people's perceptions reflect the statement, *"Wherever you go, there you are."*

No matter how much stuff you buy, no matter how many exotic vacations you take, no matter how many career changes you try, or new partners you have, your hopes and dreams and motivations, as well as your worries and insecurities and prejudices, all follow you for the ride. The proof lies in the recurring patterns that have followed you through your life, in that run of job successes, that string of relationship break-ups.

And as much as you might hope that winning Lotto, moving to the coast, or buying a red sports car will reboot your mindset, freeing you of all your old emotional baggage in an epiphany of celestial rapture, it's not going to happen. You can't escape your attitudes or your values. You can't escape yourself.

Stark and in your face but there it is.

The good news is that....you can *change yourself.* You can reset your values and replace negative limiting attitudes that hold you back with positive empowering attitudes that infuse you with an exciting future of possibility. You can change your attitudes so that every day recaptures those holiday feelings of anticipation, excitement, and being in the moment. Instead of confining these types of positive feelings to weekends and holiday trips you can have these feelings every single day. No matter where you go or what the occasion.

Because wherever you go, there you are.

Practice Happiness 14
Go to page 181

Learn to:

- ❖ Understand that your habitual thought patterns and behaviors follow you wherever you go
- ❖ Realize that you play a key role in any recurring patterns in your life
- ❖ See that the way you think and behave is reflected back at you by the world around you

15

Horoscope

Be comfortable with not knowing the future

SUNDAY MORNINGS IN OUR HOUSEHOLD are for lying in and browsing through the newspapers. After reviewing the headlines and the editorials my partner and I go straight to our favorite section – the horoscopes. She's Pisces, I'm Virgo. We have fun trying to interpret the astrologers' predictions for the week ahead:

Is this the week we're going to win the lottery?

Is this the week we will have a romantic weekend getaway?

Is this the week we will finish renovating the kitchen?

Is the business opportunity of a lifetime about to fall into our laps?

Is this the week when Doctor Who tires of journeying around the cosmos and auctions off the Tardis?

And we're not the only ones who participate in these types of discussions either. Apparently around 75 percent of the American population read horoscopes in newspapers and online, while a quarter go as far as to base tough life-changing decisions on their zodiac signs. And then there are all the other methods for predicting the future from inspecting rune stones and angel cards, to gazing at crystal balls, to reading tea leaves and tarots and fortune cookies, to reading chicken entrails (although I believe that just about anything with a gastrointestinal system will do the trick).

Do I believe in all this? No I don't, but psychologists are fully aware of the human need for reassurance. When weather patterns seem out of synch, the economy is fluctuating like a yoyo, or an individual's health appears to be at the mercy of random events, people will search for an anchor that can provide them with optimism for the day to come while at the same time serve to erase the shadow of uncertainty.

Me, I much prefer not knowing the twists and turns of life's journey. If I'd been able to read the future I probably would have missed out on dating other people, I wouldn't have rescued the stricken scuba diver on a shipwreck at a depth of 45 meters, nor had the Christmas lunch from hell when the chef did a runner. I wouldn't have any of my scars which tell you more about me than my triumphs, or have taken several jobs which, although ultimately unsuccessful, gave me the experience to land much more interesting and rewarding jobs. And I definitely wouldn't have enjoyed watching the Bourne Identity movies as much or stayed in my chair till the end of a five-setter between Roger Federer and Raphael Nadal.

If I'd taken the risk-free road through life paved with certainty I wouldn't be the person I am today. Fear of the unknown would have kept me imprisoned within my comfort zone and I'd never have grasped opportunities or believed that I could shape my own destiny. I'd never have known what I was truly capable of. I wouldn't have tasted the delicious butterfly tingles of anticipation or have felt the courageous impulsiveness of spontaneity.

And I'd have missed out on that ethereal and most exalted feeling of being *totally alive*. That feeling you get when time has ceased to exist and when all your senses sing and every fiber of your being is in the moment. Like when you abseil down a cliff for the first time, or hold your first born, or have that first kiss with the girl or boy of your dreams. Yes, I'm pleased that I can't read the future.

We each have a choice. We can endeavor to make our lives and everything in it certain or we can learn how to be comfortable with uncertainty. The first is impossible. There are just too many pieces in the puzzle that we have no control over.

Alternatively, we can learn how to ride the current and feel at ease with the unknown, and hopefully, even benefit from it.

<u>Practice Happiness 15</u>
Go to page 184

Learn to:

❖ Make change your friend
❖ Ask three questions when facing uncertainty
❖ See that feelings of discomfort often signal approaching opportunities
❖ Realize that you always have options

16

Sharks

Beware of stereotypes

SHAARRRRRK!!!

If you dropped the book and ran outside screaming at the kids to get out of the swimming pool you wouldn't be alone. You can't be too careful when it comes to these bloodthirsty killers. We need to get organized. How about a few machine gun towers at beaches and mini-submarines patrolling the coastline equipped with homing torpedoes? And our surf lifesavers should be tooled up like Rambo. I mean, masses of people are being hunted down and eaten by sharks every year, aren't they?

Well, actually no. I've just spent the past week watching Shark Week on the Discovery Channel and the statistics are very clear. On average only 25 people are killed every year by sharks. That's *worldwide*. Compare that figure with 250 people squished by elephants, 1500 stung to death by bees, 2000 zapped by lightning bolts, and 150 having their necks broken by plummeting coconuts. So, it is actually far safer to go swimming in a patch of ocean patrolled by sharks than to catch forty winks under a coconut tree. Oh, and did I mention that car accidents claim over *100,000 lives* each year around the world? Mmm.

If you want evolutionary perfection then you need look no further than sharks. They have a body that America's Cup yacht designers would drool over and sensory systems that would make military technologists weep. Just imagine if you and I were fitted out with a shark's wardrobe of gadgets. At the Olympics we could swim seven times faster than Michael Phelps. Hide-and-seek games would be a breeze as we'd be able to hear the holed up person's heartbeat from half a mile away. Getting to an outdoor theatre wouldn't be a problem as we could watch the screen from ten miles away while enjoying the smells from the Chinese restaurant in the next suburb. And to top it all off we'd never have to go to the dentist again. Ever.

Okay, so what are sharks actually doing with these superpowers if they're not flat out gobbling surfers and Hollywood actors? Much the same thing that eagles do in the skies, and that big cats do on the savannah. Sharks are the garbage collectors and quality controllers of their turf. They take their job seriously, they work long hours and they don't hold a grudge, even as a whopping *100 million* of them are killed by us each year for frivolous things like jewelry, soup and cosmetics. And they are anything but mindless killing machines – 90 percent of people attacked by sharks live to tell the tale as the shark swims away realizing that we are not part of its regular diet.

You may have guessed I'm actually a big fan of sharks. On weekends you'll find me literally falling over backwards to see them. For twenty years I've enjoyed scuba diving with sharks of all sizes from thirty foot whale shark giants to weird-looking hammerheads. And every time I gasp in wonder. One moment you are admiring this ultra-streamlined torpedo cruising languidly past and then – BANG – it explodes away from you with a flick of its tail. It's got the power of a Mack truck, the arsenal of a battleship, and the graceful moves of a ballerina – truly the Lord of the Sea. And why am I not scared? Because I know that out of four hundred and eighty species of sharks there are really only three potential nasties and even these are territorial, so if you stay out of their playground they'll leave you well alone.

And they have taught me something important too. Sharks have long been one of man's most feared bogey men with rows of glistening teeth and menacing shadows. But now, I know different.

And if most of the sharks out there are okay after all, despite all the exaggerated bad press, what other age-old stereotypes and prejudices can we give the boot?

Here are some of the more common stereotypes doing the rounds: anyone of gay persuasion must have AIDS; atheists don't have any guiding morals; people who have seen a psychologist or counselor (and freely admit to it!) must have serious mental health issues; guys only have one thing on their mind when they take a girl out on a date; people with tattoos or body piercings take drugs or are from a lower class background; all Americans practice celebrity worship and are addicted to plastic surgery; almost all vegetarians are women, and skinny women at that; middle-aged people driving sports cars are up to their necks in a full-blown midlife crisis; men over 40 who are still single are either deadbeats or are gay, while women over 40 who are still single are either married to their jobs or are gay; and all Australians are barbecue-mad exercise junkies who spend most of their time at the beach (sounds great, but alas, not true).

While stereotypes provide us with a guide for dealing with people we don't know and circumstances we are unfamiliar with they rob us of many opportunities – opportunities to learn about new things, opportunities to participate in new activities, and opportunities to be more compassionate and to recognize the humanity in each other. They also rob us of the opportunity to practice a positive outlook and experience happiness.

SHAARRRRRK!!!

Practice Happiness 16
Go to page 189

Learn to:
- ❖ Challenge stereotypes
- ❖ Look for the wonders hidden by stereotypes
- ❖ Distance yourself from those spreading harmful stereotypes

Chapter

3

Live in the Present

Savor the moment,
the birthplace of happiness

17

Bedside Prayers

Start and finish each day with gratitude

WHEN WE ARE CHILDREN WE SPEND A LOT OF TIME
kneeling beside our beds saying our night-time prayers. Truly, we
have a lot to be thankful for.

Once we start crawling we transform into midget Evil Knievals in
diapers and everyday there's a new series of survival tests we have to
pass. And pass them we must. There are cute fluffy cat tails to pull,
saucepans full of scalding hot water to grab, conveniently positioned
power-points to poke tiny fingers into, hordes of cheek-pulling
relatives to evade, and bored elder siblings plotting our demise to
hide from. It's a miracle we survive childhood at all.

Then suddenly we hit six and in an instant we kiss goodbye to our
toddler years and graduate to being a kid. Hanging out at primary
school, riding two-wheel bicycles, stocking up on candy from corner
milk-bars, staying up late on the weekends (to eight o'clock). We've
made it to the big league. And no one's telling us to say our bedtime
prayers anymore.

So we stop saying them. Because we're big people now and,
frankly, there's nothing left to be thankful for. In fact, somehow we
get it in our heads that the world now owes us.

So, the flashy bicycle with the BMX bars and air sprung forks that
was our pride and joy only a week before turns into a permanent

landscaping feature on the front lawn. And the puppy we nagged our parents for, on the condition we take responsibility for feeding it, resorts to eating the cat's food.

Then we hit our teens, a time when we're just plain ungrateful. Period. The "*me, me, me*" age of selfies and cell phones, of playing the victim card, of weaseling out of responsibilities.

But then something truly amazing happens.

Gradually, bit by bit, we begin to notice the sacrifices others make on our behalf. The long hours our dad puts in at the office to provide for the family, the time our mum spends preparing the evening meal after working all day, the basketball coach who volunteers her time on weekends, the friend who helps us with our homework during lunchtime, the bus driver who gets us to and from school safely each day. It's like a veil has been lifted from our eyes.

And we start to notice the simple, almost mundane, things in life that could so easily be taken for granted. Like feeling the sand between our toes on a beach or warming our hands over an open fire. Like waking up to the smell of freshly-ground coffee and pancakes. Or feeling like the Energizer Bunny after a gym workout.

And then there's all those everyday things that could have gone wrong but didn't. For example, have you ever picked the right cashier lane at the supermarket when all the lanes seem to be moving at a snail's pace? Have you ever pulled up at the toll booth to find the exact right change in your purse? Ever serviced your car and had the mechanic tell you that your brakes were so unroadworthy that they could have failed at any time? Ever drop a glass on the kitchen floor and have it bounce five times and not break? Or have a friend drop in unexpectedly on the one weekday you happen to be at home? Or learn that the worrying looking skin lesion on your shoulder was benign?

And, finally, there's the biggies. Those things we need to be grateful for which shape who we become as individuals and which influence how happy we feel each day. And each comes with a lesson.

Like being grateful for our families and friends who love us and support us. Which shows us the potential strength in relationships.

Being grateful for having the freedom to make choices and for being held responsible for those same choices. Which teaches us accountability and reminds us of the power we hold to change our own lives.

Being grateful for our lot in life and recognizing that many others are facing much tougher circumstances than ours. Which teaches us compassion and the joys of giving.

And being grateful for our health which gives us energy, provides a barrier against daily stresses, and makes all of our desires and dreams possible.

I still reminisce about the nights I spent kneeling beside my bed reciting my prayers. Under the benevolent gaze of my parents I learned to count my blessings.

"For these things I am eternally grateful to my mum and dad. Amen."

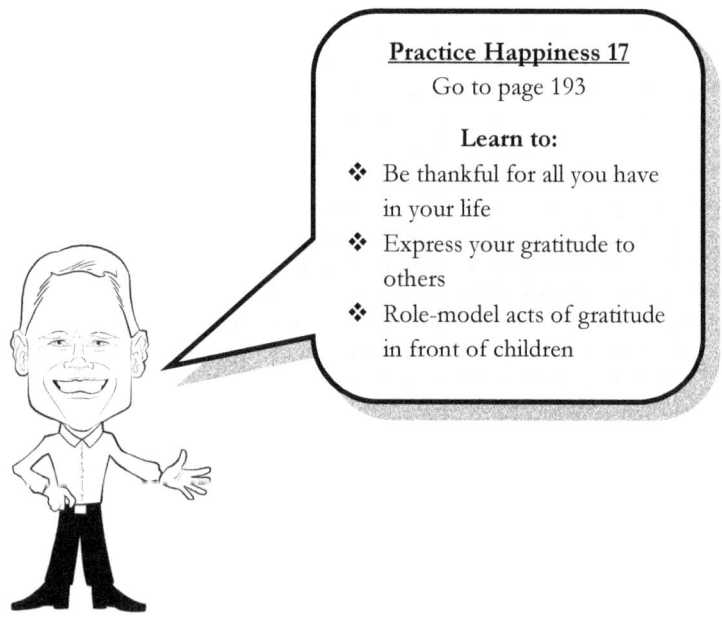

Practice Happiness 17
Go to page 193

Learn to:
- ❖ Be thankful for all you have in your life
- ❖ Express your gratitude to others
- ❖ Role-model acts of gratitude in front of children

18

Missing Socks

Reignite your curiosity of the world around you

IT'S HAPPENED AGAIN. One of my socks has vanished without a trace. No matter how careful I am when transferring the dirty laundry from the hamper into the washing machine I always end up with fewer socks than I started with. It's never shirts or trousers or handkerchiefs mind you, only socks. I've been doing a bit of research on this, asking neighbors for their theories.

The six year old girl next door who collects fairy-tale dolls is convinced the socks are being snaffled by a gang of garden gnomes who wear them as beanies on their heads.

The young lad who does my lawn mowing is an X-files fan so he blames the aliens. He reckons washing machines are actually teleporters to a far off galaxy and abducting our socks is the first step for an impending alien invasion.

Then there's the eccentric lady who lives on the corner. She favors a more divine explanation where everything is part of HIS master plan. She's got this idea that whenever we start to live the humdrum unexamined life God hits the pause button on his laptop momentarily suspending all universal laws and giving chaos and confusion free reign. Suddenly cockroaches flip onto their backs with their last gasp, shopping trolleys refuse to go where you want them to go, fluff appears in belly buttons, computers crash inexplicably when we're trying to meet deadlines, and, yes, socks disappear. She says it's God's way of gently reminding us who is really in control. And of how extraordinary our world is.

As for my own theory, a friend of mine who is a plumber gave me the official version the other day. About rinsing cycles, balanced versus unbalanced loads, and the consequences of warped agitators. And I confess I much prefer the explanations to do with garden gnomes, teleporters, and divine intervention. Mysteries are always more tantalizing when left unsolved. It's got something to do with the power of the imagination, non-stop questioning, and remaining curious.

Curiosity is one of the most neglected, but readily available, keys to happiness. When we are curious about something we are fully alive in the present moment. Plus, we are encouraged to look in new directions and engage with the world in more meaningful ways. Every discovery and advancement ultimately came about as a result of someone being curious which fired up their imagination leading to eureka moments of insight. Curiosity also makes relationships more satisfying as we take a greater interest in others.

A common affliction of the 21st century sees young people (and some not so young) complain of chronic boredom. The good news is that a curious person can't be bored. Whether you're waiting for a doctor's appointment, are stuck in a traffic jam, or are stranded inside on a rainy day, if you're curious about your world you will never be bored. EVER. I guarantee it.

Curiosity makes you want to put on your shoes and charge out the door to interact with the world.

I think I'll head off for a walk right now. With different colored socks.

Practice Happiness 18
Go to page 196

Learn to:

❖ Reignite your curiosity about this amazing world

❖ See the extraordinary in the ordinary – by being a child, a tourist, a photographer, an anthropologist, an archaeologist, an adventurer, and an alien

19

Makeovers

Remain young at heart

MAKEOVERS ARE WHAT EVERYONE'S TALKING about nowadays. I remember when makeovers meant tinkering away on a rusting Holden in the corner of the yard and repainting a tired old chest of drawers in the attic. Well, not anymore.

Flick on the television today and you'll be buried beneath an avalanche of makeover shows. The most popular shows look at personal makeovers. Viewers are told that in just a few hours a crack team of plastic surgeons and cosmetic artists with a snippity-tuck here and some spray-on tan there will restore the client's pasty wrinkled face to its former glory. We watch with baited breath and gasp with envy at the results.

I reckon I'd qualify for a TV makeover. I could try one of those massive Hollywood-style facelifts with the bee sting lips and the wind tunnel blasted look. But my partner wouldn't be sure whether I was ecstatic or enraged. The body builder look with the six-pack tummy, bulging biceps and tree trunk legs would be great for the ego. But then I'd start thinking I was Arnold Schwarzenegger and have an identity crisis. A few Celtic tattoos on the arms and legs might make me seem more intriguing and worldly. Although I've already got scars aplenty from my travels and each has its own interesting story. And the shattered hairdo look with the mop of short blonde spikes set in cement-hardening putty won't cut it either. Why spend a fortune on hairstyling when I can have grey distinguished looking streaks for free?

Truth be told I actually know what sort of makeover I want. Not one that keeps me *looking* young but one that keeps me *feeling* young.

And I'll know if I got my money's worth because:

I'll try to make a game of everything I do (except when eating at the dining table, of course).

I'll race the kids to the kitchen to lick the eggbeaters clean when a chocolate cake is being made.

I'll run up the down escalator in the department stores.

I'll stop whatever I'm doing to listen to stories about dinosaurs, Big Foot, or the Bermuda Triangle.

Whenever I'm in a crowd watching fireworks I'll be the one gasping the loudest.

I'll think nothing of dancing a jig at the supermarket when the mood takes me.

When there's a flash of lightning I'll count off the miles before the peal of thunder 1....2....3.....BOOM!!

I'll never let myself get bored. Never ever.

I'll remember that the toys that were the most fun were the ones that didn't require batteries – because they were powered by one's imagination.

I'll use the same sunny optimism and dogged willpower that helped me learn to ride a bike and climb trees to conquer my fear of kids' video games and Blackberry instructions.

On drizzly summer days I'll think nothing of getting out and exercising or going for a nice long walk.

I'll go into a hypnotic trance when I hear the Mr. Whippy jingle signaling the approach of the ice cream van up the street.

And no matter what I'm busy doing there'll only ever be one thing on my mind – whatever I'm busy doing.

Now *that's* the type of makeover I want. A makeover that allows me to remain young at heart. One that gets me bouncing out of bed every morning in anticipation of adventures and imaginings. Where I don't take life too seriously and I laugh every chance I get. And where limiting thoughts, like fears and regrets, that wrinkle the soul and shackle the growing spirit are replaced by optimism and self-compassion.

If you know of a reality TV show that offers this type of makeover, sign me up.

Practice Happiness 19
Go to page 198

Learn to:
- ❖ Remain young at heart
- ❖ Celebrate something every day
- ❖ Challenge expectations associated with your age

20

Kisses

The best things in life are moments

THEY FIRST DID IT IN BOOKS IN INDIA 1,500 YEARS ago. Before long the Romans were doing it behind closed doors. By the Middle Ages they were playing games at county fairs doing it. In the 20th century people started packing movie theatres to watch film stars do it. Then international soccer players began doing it after scoring a goal. And recently, a whopping 5,327 couples made history doing it on Valentine's Day.

Kissing. It's more fashionable today than ever before. Everyone seems to be doing it every chance they get, right? Well, I came across a newspaper story the other day exploring just that question and it got me thinking about some of the most memorable kissing moments we enjoy in our lives.

Like our first romantic kiss. I can still remember mine. I was sixteen and my best friend managed to hook me up with his ex-girlfriend for our school's end-of-year dance. (Doesn't sound very romantic I know, but hey, I was an innocent adolescent). It wasn't until the very end of the night that we actually kissed. After a brief period of feinting and parrying reminiscent of two wrestlers sizing each other up at the start of a bout I pursed my lips and, like a stork bobbing for fish, went for it. CRUNCH. Not to be outdone we unlocked molars and after negotiating a few Jim Carey facial contortions we enjoyed a moment of exquisite bliss when our lips melted together. Sigh. *(This is my recollection of events and I'm sticking to it.)*

Anyway, that first kiss sets in motion a train of wonderful romantic kisses that we get to enjoy with our special someone. At the marriage ceremony we seal the deal by fusing our souls together with the most sublime of kisses. Then there are teasing kisses when leaving each other to go to work, whispering kisses while watching one another sleep, cheeky kisses to interrupt each other mid-sentence, candy kisses when sharing treats, electric kisses after rubbing socked feet back and forth on the rug, rollicking open-mouthed kisses when hungry for love, and long lingering passionate kisses in front of the fire.

Amazingly, an abundance of these kisses often coincides with the arrival of new family members. These little bundles of joy bring with them their own unique set of glorious kisses. There are bubbly fun kisses on rounded baby tummies and soft fluttery goodnight kisses when we tuck them into bed and healing kisses for tiny cuts and grazes. And lots and lots of spontaneous kisses to remind them how much we love them. Then our children grow up and start creating their very own kissing memories.

So, back to the newspaper story I was telling you about. The one that looked at how much time we actually spend kissing. Researchers have found that, while we spend three months of our lives brushing our teeth and a whole six months sitting in the smallest room in the house, we only spend two weeks – a measly two weeks – of our lives kissing.

It turns out that life's not one big smorgasbord of kisses after all. I guess that just goes to show that each kiss is extra special. And that it is the *moments in life* that are to be treasured.

We're blessed that our lives are full of so many special moments. Like the morning you received your university acceptance letter in the mail. And years later the day you graduated from university. Or the day you were handed the keys to your first car. Or the moment you proposed and she said, "Yes!" Or the moment you learnt you were going to be a father. Or when you heard about that fantastic job opportunity. Or the last time you looked into the eyes of your faithful pet dog. And the list goes on. The moment you jumped out of a perfectly good plane at 10,000 feet; the moment you put the final stroke on the painting you had devoted a year to; the glorious lunar eclipse you witnessed when camping in the bush; the moment you felt God enter your life; the moment you looked down at the scales and realized you had reached your goal weight; your first day working on your dream job; the charity event when you first discovered the enormous satisfaction derived from helping others; the last time you kissed one of your parents before they passed away. Or maybe the day you made the conscious decision to overhaul parts of your life so you could be happy.

Moments. At the end of the day that's all you have. You can appreciate them and make the most of them or you can let them slip through your fingers like sand.

You're having a moment *right now.*

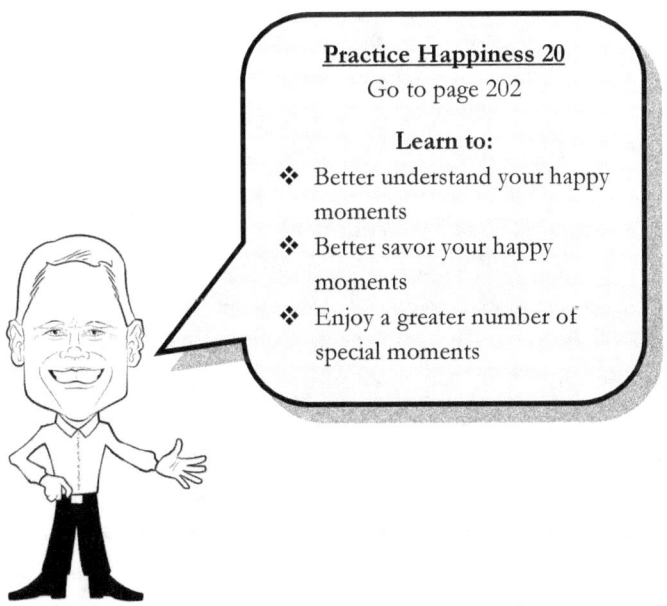

Practice Happiness 20
Go to page 202

Learn to:
- ❖ Better understand your happy moments
- ❖ Better savor your happy moments
- ❖ Enjoy a greater number of special moments

21

Driving an MG

Savor the moment by practicing mindfulness

EVER SINCE I WAS A KID I WANTED AN MGB Roadster. A red one with a black soft-top. You know, with the goggle-eyed headlamps, the cheesy front grille, and the gunslinger spoke wheels. *Oh yeahhh.* I'd go into a trance and start salivating whenever one burbled past. I was hooked. And then just last September, after forty long years, I fulfilled a kid's dream and I bought one.

From the moment you slide down into the cockpit – after successfully completing a contortionist routine rivaling Cirque du Soleil – you realize you're in for an experience. To begin with, you're low to the ground. Very low. Your pet Dachshund is peering down at you through the side window in bewilderment. In front of you the dashboard is decorated with a pleasing array of toggle switches and dials which make satisfying clicks and whirring sounds. And you're confronted with such luxury comforts as wind up windows and a glove box (believe me, a big deal back in the mid-1960s).

Then it's time to start the MGB. This requires patience and compassion. She is 50 years old after all. After several minutes of idling, accompanied by a flurry of gulps from the fuel pump and the odd geriatric burp and fart, she is completely awake and is purring like a kitten.

Once out on the city streets you'll find that she can be a bit temperamental. If you're a fraction late when going up through the gears she emits a throaty rasp and if, god forbid, you accidentally mistake the second gear for fourth – LOOK OUT – she will scream at you in protest. Fortunately, she doesn't bear a grudge. Crossing speed humps that look like small hills tests your nerve and throwing coins into an automatic toll booth requires a well executed basketball hook shot. Because she lacks a chassis every bump on the road threatens to shake loose one of your teeth and so you're always trying to dodge potholes and tiptoe across rough surfaces. And when waiting at traffic lights on a steep slope total concentration is needed as you juggle the accelerator and handbrake, while keeping one eye on the lights, the other on the bumper bar of the car looming up behind you.

And then you hit the open highway. As you accelerate to 30....35....40 miles per hour, your finger hovers over the switch that will engage the overdrive turning your MGB into a turbo-propelled Batmobile with flames shooting out of the rear exhaust. (That's how I see it anyway). *And then you flick the switch.* Instantly the guttural growl is replaced by a finely-tuned burble and the cacophony of vibrating squeaks and cheeps that had dogged you through the streets of suburbia fade away. Cruising along with the wind rifling your hair, the sun on your face, the crackle of the exhaust when your foot kisses the accelerator, you find yourself smiling like a village idiot. Older motorists toot and wave and the younger generation stare in admiration. And young kids salivate.

You may be asking yourself why I drive an MGB with all of its obvious idiosyncrasies and frailties when I could be in a contemporary vehicle packed with onboard computers, power steering, air conditioning and the like?

The reason is that the MGB is a time capsule that demands my full attention. And I love that. At first I used to *watch* the revs on the dial, then I learned to *listen* to the revs, and eventually I was able to *feel* the revs. You don't just drive an MGB. It's the every-inch classic motoring experience that captures your body, mind, heart and soul. It forces you to be IN the moment. And that's what I want – the full *in-*

the-moment experience.

There's a word for this type of experience where you give your complete attention to the present moment in a non-judgmental way. Buddhists call it *mindfulness*. Being mindful has many benefits. Focusing on only one thing heightens your powers of concentration while also giving you greater self-awareness of your body, thoughts and emotions. This means that you can nip self-defeating thoughts and judgments in the bud leading to greater compassion for yourself and for others. Also, because your attention is not being distracted by competing interests you will feel calmer, more at peace, and will waste less energy.

You only have to look at the joy on the faces of children when they are playing to appreciate the pure happiness that comes from immersing yourself in a single activity, free of expectations and judgments.

I'm off for a drive in the MGB. Care to join me?

Practice Happiness 21
Go to page 203

Learn to:
* Be more relaxed
* Keep your mind free of judgments
* Keep your thoughts aligned with your behaviors
* Become a more effective listener

22

Breathing

Breathing is the easiest way to stay in the present

THE FAVORITE GAME AT POOL PARTIES when I was a child was seeing who could hold their breath the longest. My record was around one and a half minutes. Not bad. A Frenchman Stephane Mifsud is a regular fish with the world record of 11 minutes 35 seconds. Wow! Humpback whales can stay under for 45 minutes. But no one comes close to the Wood Frog of North America. He can hold his breath for a whopping 3 months when hibernating during freezing cold winters.

We start holding our breath early on. Especially whenever we're anxious or distressed. When we're sent to bed without dinner, receive a scolding for dropping the milk, or are picked on in the playground we instinctively pull up the drawbridge – *"Hup"* and stop breathing. All our muscles tense up and we get that deer-caught-in-the-headlights look. And we start fast shallow breathing.

We've all seen our fair share of fast shallow breathers. Nervous plane passengers with hands welded to armrests. Apprehensive interview candidates tapping out the opening theme to *I Dream of Jeanie* with their feet. People turning themselves into human pretzels to avoid watching injections with needles. Chastised husbands and wives reprimanded by their partners in public (*a slam dunk for guaranteeing hyperventilation*).

For the most part, it's a normal reaction to an experience we consider stressful. The fight or flight response at work. Our body is preparing itself to either meet the source of stress head-on or get the heck out of there. Then, once the initial unsettling moment has passed we're meant to resume normal breathing – slooow deeeeep breaths, or diaphragmatic breathing – the factory settings we were born with. A friend of mine who is a yoga instructor tells me this whole process is quite normal.

The moment of truth comes, she says, as we start having more and more anxiety-ridden experiences. The breathing patterns we use in response to these experiences can quickly turn into a habit. Unless we have our very own breathing guru on hand to remind us to return to our factory settings we run the risk of living our lives stuck in shallow breathing mode. *(Other bad habits contribute to our poor breathing style including poor posture, smoking, multitasking, lack of exercise, restrictive clothing, fatty diets, and slouching in front of computers and TV screens.)*

The big problem with long-term shallow breathing is that it robs us of the present. When we're shallow breathing we're more likely to be wrestling with future worries or past regrets. Our thoughts are not in the present. Instead of giving our complete attention to our friend, part of our mind is listening while the other part is anguishing over our upcoming weekend plans. Instead of being alert for new business opportunities at the conference, we're replaying in our minds the quarrel we had earlier with another motorist. Instead of savoring the moment while sharing a romantic bath with our darling partner, we're mentally rehearsing our speech to the board.

The point is we can only act in the present. Because that's where our physical body is. And so we need to be able to *keep our thoughts in the present*. Which means breathing slowly and deeply.

Just think about all those marvelous opportunities we are given every day to practice the skill of diaphragmatic breathing. There are bank queues and supermarket check-out queues and telephone call waiting queues. There are dental and doctor's waiting rooms. We can always expect traffic jams. There may be misunderstandings to sort out with work colleagues. And – hey, this is the real world – we can expect to have arguments with our partner, and with our family and friends.

So whenever an unexpected crisis occurs or you just have a spare moment in your day hit the slow deep breathing button. It's the most valuable tool you will have for reconnecting with the present. And best of all, you carry it around with you everywhere you go.

<u>Practice Happiness 22</u>
Go to page 208

Learn to:
- ❖ Identify your own breathing style
- ❖ Breathe properly for optimal health
- ❖ Feel less stressed through proper breathing
- ❖ Realize that you mimic others' breathing patterns

23

Heart Transplant Recipient

Live each day as if it could be your last

EVERY COUNTRY HAS ITS OWN ICONS. The Statue of Liberty in the USA, the La Marseillaise national anthem of France, the Lion of England, the kangaroo of Australia. National symbols that make you teary-eyed, swell your chest with feelings of pride, and which motivate you to dig deeper for that extra effort when you think you've given your all.

However, the icon that does all this for me you won't find on any official list. It's a woman. And she didn't invent anything. She didn't write bestsellers, traverse the North Pole or win a swag of Olympic gold medals. She lived. That's all. But it's enough. She REALLY....LIVED.

In 1970, at the age of 14, Fiona Coote was your regular farm girl living out in the boonies when she contracted tonsillitis. Within a month her life was turned upside down when her heart became severely weakened. So much so, that she had to have a heart transplant. Up to this time all the previous heart transplant recipients had died within months of surgery. Every sickness, even a minor cold, was viewed as a possible sign of heart rejection. The best possible prognosis gave her five years to live – up to her 21st birthday.

She changed her lifestyle, adopted a healthier diet, and started a regular exercise regime. She was always in the public eye.

The weeks and months passed. She began using her celebrity status to promote healthy food products and begin working for charitable organizations.

The years passed. She became more and more involved in community work, particularly in raising public awareness of heart disease and in raising funds for seriously and terminally ill children.

In 1993, at the age of 23, when asked whether she lived in constant fear of her heart stopping, she said, "No. You've got to get out there and enjoy it. You have an obligation to the person who died so you could live." When asked what was most important to her, she replied, "Family and friends. Mostly enjoyment. Just being happy!" And when asked if she was indeed happy, she laughed and said, "I'm very happy. I laugh a lot. After all I've been through, if I were to be miserable, what a terrible waste of time."

What an extraordinary and courageous woman. And what a wonderful recipe for happiness – heaps of laughter, a healthy dollop of gratitude, a love of family and friends, an upbeat attitude.

Makes me wonder how I would live my life differently if I knew I was living on borrowed time, if I was told that any day, any week could be my last. Would I take more risks in my professional life? Would I take more risks in my personal life? Would I love more? Would I give more? Would I laugh more? Cry more? Would I *live* more?

Which makes me think about those stories we hear on the news of people who reinvent their lives after having near-death experiences from natural disasters or life-threatening illnesses. Being granted a second shot at life motivates them to reflect upon their past life. And they shake their heads in amazement at the way they were so preoccupied with the future.

So they resolve to live more in the present. They become less obsessed with material possessions and far more interested in displaying compassion and gratitude towards others. They make a point of searching for their life purpose and they develop a perennial sense of wonder for the simple things in life. They decide to make the most of each day. And not to wait until the next promotion comes along, or the kids have left home, or the doctor issues a health ultimatum. But to live NOW.

You know, before their near-death experience these people did what we all do – they lived their lives in a state of complacency as if all the days in the world were still to come. Little did they know.

Come to think of it, little do *we all know*....

And what of Fiona Coote?

She's still going strong. At the ripe old age of 44 she continues to throw down the gauntlet to the rest of us. By living each day as if it could be her last.

Practice Happiness 23
Go to page 212

Learn to:
- ❖ Imagine your likely future if you continue living as you are now
- ❖ See that the perfect time to grab that opportunity is always now
- ❖ Laugh more every day

24

Spring Cleaning

Clean out your emotional cupboards

SPRING CLEANING CAN BE VERY LIBERATING. You get to throw open windows, give rugs a decent flogging, round up herds of dust bunnies, rummage through boxes of unused stuff. It's a great chance to start afresh. Like resetting your computer from scratch. There's less clutter, more space, you know where things are. It just feels so darn good.

And if you're going to do a thorough job why not spring clean all that emotional junk that's been building up as well. The closets full of prejudices. The attics full of painful memories. The basements full of old grudges. While physical junk clutters up our home, emotional junk clutters up our hearts. It causes us to stagnate in the past, instead of moving forward with our lives. I say, let's make this a spring clean to remember.

Top of the to-do list is cleaning. Actual getting-your-hands-dirty cleaning. Dusting knick-knacks and light fixtures is one thing. Cleaning toilet bowls and drainpipes is something else altogether. If we don't keep on top of these the grime will build up pretty quickly leading to nasty stains or blockages.

It's like that with our everyday attitudes. Particularly any negative attitudes. They weigh heavily on our hearts and over time if left unchecked can become emotional gunk habits. We need to flush this gunk away. Gunk like judgments and prejudices that limit our creativity. Flush it down the sink with a good dose of tolerance. And what about the gunk of hiding behind past disappointments instead of taking future risks? Or refusing to accept blame while always painting ourselves as the victim. Yep, flush 'em all with an undiluted mixture of self-responsibility, self-confidence and self-love. And how about the real drain-clogging muck where we convince ourselves that the grass is always greener on the other side of the fence? Yuck. Nasty, stinky, putrid stuff. Flush it with a mixture of two parts count your blessings, one part mindfulness.

Flushed with success (so to speak), it's time to do something about those things that we rarely use but seem unable to part with. Like the clothes that haven't been worn in years, and the bottle of Paul Newman jam in the kitchen cupboard that's so out of date it was probably bottled by Paul Newman himself, the remote that doesn't seem to operate anything in the house but just sits there on the coffee table, and the pile of old yellowed linen in the closet that's home to a squadron of moths. Even though we're managing perfectly well without the stuff that little voice tells us to hang on to it. Just in case. So we leave the stuff where it is.

Which is what we do when we hold a grudge. Someone hurt us in the past and we don't want to forget what happened. We want to be ready to repay the pain they inflicted upon us should the opportunity come along. Somehow we think that would make us feel better. So we keep the grudge in our back pocket. Just in case. But all this does is allow feelings of anger and distrust to fester keeping us chained to the past and suspicious of the future. If we wish to move forward with our lives this emotional garbage has to get the heave-ho. I say, put that grudge in a big cardboard box and place it on the curb for the compost collectors. Know that it's about to be recycled and both you and the person who hurt you are to be the beneficiaries of organically grown forgiveness.

And to complete the jumble, there are the relics gathering dust in our garage or attic. Things that we only rediscover when we're moving house. Ancient treasures like football swap cards, and decades-old birthday cards, high school blazers and communion dresses, and shoeboxes full of old dusty cassette tapes. And stuff full of painful memories like letters from previous lovers or wedding pictures from a previous marriage that we hideaway at the bottom of boxes. We keep all this stuff solely for sentimental reasons.

Similarly, in the garage and attic of our minds is where we store the emotional baggage of our deepest and most intense memories. Even though we rarely look at this junk, it is still there taking up head space and coloring the way we look at our future. Junk like childhood hurts that breed resentment, and past failures like broken marriages and job losses that leave a legacy of bitterness and guilt. And regrets of things we feel we should have done or not done. Replaying these in our minds only succeeds in anchoring us to the past and perpetuating a mistaken belief that our fate is dictated by our past experiences. I say, put it all in a trailer, take it to the tip, and toss it. Then clean your hands thoroughly with an antibacterial soap of self-forgiveness, compassion for others, and hope.

Once you rid yourself of emotional garbage your heart and mind is freed from the shackles of the past and becomes open to all the possibilities of the present. *Each day represents a fresh slate* full of a whole new set of opportunities for love and hope and the chance to redesign your future.

So I say, roll up your sleeves and let's get busy cleaning.

<u>Practice Happiness 24</u>
Go to page 216

Learn to:

❖ Forgive yourself for any past wrongs
❖ Let go of grudges against others
❖ Realize that you are responsible for your own emotional baggage
❖ Spring clean any emotional baggage in your relationships

25

Clearance Sale

You don't need more stuff to be happy

'HURRY. TODAY ONLY!" "Massive clearance. Must go!"

Boxing Day sales hoopla. When talking about sales mania this is the big one. The World Series. A couple of years ago my partner and I went to see what we had been missing. I was riding shotgun and doubling as a parter-of-the-seas. She would point me in the right direction and off we'd go, me shimmying my way through the masses, her clinging to my back like a limpet. Every table was a rugby scrum of stretched arms and desperate fingers. Changing rooms were knee-deep in tossed garments. And cashier counters looked like the floor at the stock exchange with frenzied shoppers holding aloft their bargains while frantically waving their credit cards. With Russell Crowe as crowd controller it could have been the coliseum in Rome with shoppers for gladiators. This bargain hunting gig is not for the faint hearted.

And what of the bargains? Are they must-haves? Do they make a difference in the household? Probably not. Once our victorious shopping gladiators return home and the thrill of the bargain has worn off, most of the goodies soon find themselves confined to cupboards. Or to storage sheds – of which there has been an explosion in recent years.

Shoppers are seduced by the price, not because of the usefulness or value of an item. It's all part of the more-is-better world we live in. The world where buy-one-get-one-free is the modern battle cry of rampant consumerism.

Every time we drive past a billboard, power up our computer, or turn on the TV we're bombarded with messages telling us to *want more*. According to Big Brother we should:

Be earning a salary with *more* dollars and a job with *more* status.

Be married to a husband who is *more* manly or to a wife who has *more* curves.

Live in a house with *more* rooms and drive a car with *more* gizmos and gadgets.

Own a tablet with *more* memory, a Smartphone with *more* features, and log into a Facebook account that has hundreds *more* friends.

Take holiday packages with *more* add-on trips and lug around a camera with *more* accessories.

And stop for a coffee at Starbucks on the way home and order the mug that's big enough to drown yourself in because – what the heck – it's only $1....*more*.

The message is that having more will make us happier. When we are constantly focused on wanting more, be it money or friends or stuff or even time itself, our thoughts and our energies are in the future. We are not fully engaged in the present. Telling ourselves "I'll be happy WHEN I get that more of something" is pinning our happiness on a future circumstance. It is an illusion because tomorrow never arrives.

Also, there is the danger that we will not allow ourselves to be happy until we obtain the *something* more. And there is always something more. A car with more features, a woman that is more beautiful, a better paid job. The thing that we crave is always just out of reach guaranteeing that we remain never completely happy or content.

This is why so often after scrimping and saving for months to buy that home cinema system or after counting the hours till that hot date people are surprised when they feel hollow or let down afterwards. They relish the anticipatory feelings of excitement leading up to their goal but fail to capitalize on fully enjoying the present moment when the moment actually arrives. And then, in an attempt to combat their feelings of emptiness, they quickly buy something else or rush to set up another date (an e-dating addiction). One anticlimax seems to follow another.

The remedy is not to *stop* wanting more but to enjoy and be thankful for what we have NOW. We need to put our entire heart and soul into making the most of the material possessions and the relationships we have today.

The grass is always greener on *this* side of the fence. Why? Because this side of the fence is where we are right now. In the present. We can't change the future but we can change the present.

And the present is where we will experience the happiness we seek.

> **Practice Happiness 25**
> Go to page 220
>
> **Learn to:**
> ❖ Check if having more things aligns with your life purpose and values
> ❖ Ask yourself these questions when you feel the urge to buy something
> ❖ Savor experiences that are free or cost very little

Chapter

4

Live a Fully Connected Life

Enjoy more meaningful
and fulfilling relationships

26

Crickets

E-Messages are no substitution for face-to-face conversations

DON'T YOU JUST LOVE BALMY SUMMER EVENINGS in the backyard? Those evenings of outdoor barbecues and just-watered flower beds, where stars wink at you through silhouetted trees, and the air is heavy with the trills and chirps of an assembly of insect orchestras. You may not have realized it but for weeks on end you have had a front row seat to a nightly dusk performance of the world's greatest serenader.

I'm referring to the humble mole cricket. His job is to attract a mate in a garden that's a frenzied cauldron of love tunes, a bit like you trying to get the attention of someone twenty meters away at a Deep Purple concert. *But he has an edge.* He has his own musical instrument – a singing burrow. While digging his little opera house he constantly tests the acoustics by rubbing his wings together like a violinist. When the burrow is finely tuned and ready he presses his wings up against the ceiling and launches into song. CRICK-CRICK, CRICK-CRICK, CRICK-CRICK. The burrow amplifies the sound an astonishing two hundred times. Topside, circling female suitors listen to his love song. If one likes what she hears she visits his burrow and if she likes what she sees she moves in. His engineering genius means that he never has to leave home to get a girl.

We have a singing burrow of sorts too. But instead of serenading passers-by with a loudhailer from the kitchen window we use a computer to broadcast our song. In fact, we have become dependent on our burrows for much more than simply finding a mate. And now we have made our burrows portable.

Portable computers in the form of tablets and Smartphones have become the latest fashion accessory accompanying people wherever they go. On public transport, in offices, on university campuses, in parks, in coffee shops, at restaurants, even around the family dining table everyone is hunched over their computers (just like the mole cricket). They're all busy conversing with someone else.

Wait! Scratch that! They're not conversing, but *connecting* with someone else.

Because there's the rub. Connecting with 1,000 Facebook friends is just that, and only that – connecting. Being plugged in 24/7 is compelling, and addictive for some, because it creates the illusion that we are always being heard and that we are never alone.

How often have you seen partners at a restaurant or friends in a pub desperately reach for their Blackberrys and iPhones when there's a lull in the conversation? Uncomfortable with silence and not knowing how to develop the conversation further they instantly metamorphose into a technology-savvy turtle with shoulders rounded forward, head tucked in, and eyes glued to a screen. Frantically they type an sms message that reads something like, "SOS. Can't think of anything to say. Help!"

And that's okay. It's called the art of conversation for a reason. Being able to initiate and then maintain a conversation takes work. It's a skill that requires patience, compassion, and the ability to see the world from someone else's perspective.

Face-to-face conversations may be messy and unedited, and yes, sometimes boring, but they achieve a spontaneity and richness of communication that cannot be matched by a string of text messages. When talking to someone in person you are fully engaged and the chances of miscommunication are reduced because you can respond to voice tone and body language. This all leads to a much greater depth and quality in relationships.

Our parents and our grandparents knew this and were master conversationalists. Of course, they had to be – they didn't have devices they could hide behind. They lived in the days when people walked with their heads held high and actively sought out eye contact with others. This guaranteed talking. And lots of it.

The mole cricket does have a better ear for acoustics than us and he probably keeps a neater house too but we do have something over him. For all his virtuoso abilities he is homebound and at the whims of others for company, while we are free to enjoy face-to-face talks anywhere and at anytime. Simply by looking....UP.

Practice Happiness 26
Go to page 227

Learn to:
❖ Lay down rules and boundaries at the start of important conversations
❖ Practice the most important rule for maintaining a conversation
❖ Demonstrate effective conversation skills to your children

27

Pied Piper of Amsterdam

Remember the Golden Rule

ONE OF THE ALL-TIME BEST OLYMPIC MOMENTS. It's Quarterfinal Day of the singles sculling competition at the 1928 Olympic Games in Amsterdam. One of the favorites to win the event is Bobby Pearce, the Australian champion rower. Pearce hails from a family with a long and distinguished sporting pedigree. He was born to scull. As such, the expectations weighing upon his broad shoulders are colossal.

However, standing in his way is Savrin, the French champion.

After an explosive start the two scullers settle into a workman-like rhythm and are soon eating up the 2000 meter course. Midway through the race Bobby is rowing powerfully with a relaxed stroking style. With every sweep of the blades the wind ruffles his blonde hair and his boat shoots forward on the glass-smooth water. Everything is going to plan. He's confident of victory.

But then above the roar of the crowd he hears it. Someone is shouting frantically on the banks of the canal behind him. He risks a quick peek over his shoulder and sees a large group of children pointing vigorously at something in the water. He follows their gaze and is astonished to see directly in his path – but not in the Frenchman's – *a mother duck with her ducklings swimming slowly in single file across the canal.*

Bobby doesn't even flinch. He immediately drops his oars in the water applying the brakes to his boat giving the family of ducks time to complete their crossing. And giving the Frenchman time to open up a five-length lead.

Surely the race is lost? Or is it? Digging deep he lifts the tempo of his strokes and overtakes the Frenchman in the closing stages to win the race. The gold medal and the title of Olympic champion are his.

And the story doesn't end there. The children who were on the banks of the canal that day to witness Bobby's wonderful gesture in the heat of competition tell other children. Who, in turn, tell other children. His selfless act captures their hearts completely and for the rest of the Games the children of Holland follow him wherever he goes. In Olympic sporting folklore he is remembered as the Pied Piper of Amsterdam.

And the point of this story? It's about words like respect and kindness and compassion. It's about treating others the way you would like to be treated – *the Golden Rule*. Most importantly, it's about taking that extra step of actually acting upon one's empathy for others. That's what Bobby did when he dropped his oars after seeing the reactions on the children's faces. These are the moments when the Gods watching from a heavenly stadium leap to their feet and cheer "Score one for mankind!"

The seeds of the Golden Rule are being planted every day in the minds' of our children at home, at school, and on the playground. We exhort our children to be honest and to respect each other. We encourage them to share their toys and help each other up after falling over. We praise them when they take responsibility for their actions and when they volunteer without having to be asked. And we hope that they will do the right thing even when no one is looking.

These are valuable lessons which will follow our children throughout their lives. Of course, the litmus test of how well the lesson will be learnt depends on our own actions and whether we – you and I – actually practice the Golden Rule each day. Whether we make a habit of actively looking for opportunities to help our fellow man. Whether we pay compliments and say nice things to others to brighten their day. Whether we listen to others even though it may be an inconvenient time for us to do so. And whether we are compassionate enough to forgive others who wrong us.

This is the litmus test because we are the children of yesteryear. Just like Bobby Pearce.

Practice Happiness 27
Go to page 231

Learn to:
- ❖ Look for opportunities to help others
- ❖ Choose to say nice things to people
- ❖ Own up to your mistakes and practice self-compassion
- ❖ Role-model the Golden Rule to children

28

Melbourne Cup Horse Race

Celebrate humanity by talking with strangers every day

AUSTRALIA COMES TO A COMPLETE STANDSTILL for three minutes on the same day every year. It's been going on for the past one hundred and fifty years. And it's about to happen again.

Come early afternoon people all across the land stop what they're doing. Politicians cut short debates, construction workers down tools, teachers interrupt classes and there is an orderly stampede towards any available televisions and radios. Then, on the stroke of ten minutes after two, Eastern Standard Time, the entire nation catches its breath....before screaming itself hoarse for three full minutes. After which everyone calmly returns to their jobs.

The reason?

A horse race. Just a horse race. *Or is it?*

From the moment the sun rises on Melbourne Cup Day people start acting a bit weird. Think of the movie *"Invasion of the Body Snatchers"* where folks are replaced with alien cloned replicas who behave totally out of character and you've pretty much got the picture. All across the country people walk straight up to total strangers and strike up lively conversations. This happens in the streets, on buses, in queues, in elevators, even in public washrooms. Incredibly, overnight everyone becomes a horse racing aficionado with opinions on racetrack surfaces, horse personality types, and the dietary habits of jockeys.

All the conventions of proper dress sense are turned on their head as well. Sequined mini-skirts, tuxedos with psychedelic board shorts, and hats of the make-you-sit-up-and-gasp variety are all the fashion. In fact, the hats worn at the racecourse are so fantastically monstrous that the horses, already highly strung, have to be blinkered to prevent them galloping the wrong way around the track. And there are picnics and office luncheons everywhere. In backyards, warehouses, car parks and racetracks revelers party like there's no tomorrow.

Now bear in mind that all this happens in a country where most Australians are hard pressed picking one end of a horse from the other, let alone trying to pick a winner by deciphering form guides and unraveling the complexities of betting odds. Which begs the question – how does a nation with such a paltry understanding of the sport of kings become so spellbound by a horse race?

I'm mulling over this while sitting in Melbourne's city square on Cup Day with a thousand other people, all staring up at a huge video screen. The sea of faces around me is a snapshot of Australia's diverse multicultural fabric. People of all complexions – fair, swarthy, tawny, ebony, rose, olive, peaches-and-cream – from all corners of the globe. All come together for a horse race.

Many of them are holding aloft cut-out horses on ice-cream sticks and as the minutes countdown to the start of the race the forest of paper horses is being jiggled ever more furiously. On the screen the horses and jockeys are being introduced while at the same time streams of betting odds crawl across the bottom of the screen.

As I'm trying to make sense of this gobbledygook I feel a tug on one of my trouser legs. A young Sikh lad wearing a black turban is looking up at me and asks in a matter-of-fact voice, "Excuse me, what do all those numbers on the screen mean?"

"I have absolutely no idea," I reply.

"Do we need to know any of that stuff?"

"No, we don't," I say. "Once we pick a horse we just hope it wins."

"Good. I'm feeling really lucky today. I think my horse is going to win."

"Good for you. Maybe it will."

And finally, he says, "This is heaps of fun, isn't it?"

"It sure is," I agree wholeheartedly. We both smile and then look back at the screen, his paper horse resuming its frenetic dance.

And suddenly I have the answer to my question. The race is so popular because it gives people a chance to look beyond their status, race, or religion and bask in the fellowship of humanity. This is the common denominator and everyone from complete novices to seasoned gamblers, from Buddhists to atheists, from high court judges to road workers, and from teenagers to grandparents can come together and celebrate as one.

Call me old fashioned but I still prefer a face-to-face chinwag with a complete stranger to scrolling through a list of virtual Facebook friends any day. And I'm not alone. I'm convinced that the resurgence in interest in national events like the Melbourne Cup and Anzac Day is due to people craving opportunities to come together and reconnect. At a time when more and more people are living alone and common traditional methods of personal interaction are being usurped by technology, simply turning to the person sitting next to you on the train and saying hello is at the very heart of what it means to be human.

That's why I'm proposing a *World Talk to Strangers Day*. It will improve people's communication skills, promote interpersonal trust, melt away feelings of loneliness, and help all of us develop more compassion for our fellow man.

And instead of it being an annual event I'm suggesting we make it a monthly event (secretly I'm gunning for it as a daily event, but one step at a time). But first, in order for it to be recognized by the United Nations, we need to trial it in our communities. I'm off to the park for a stroll to get the ball rolling.

<u>Practice Happiness 28</u>
Go to page 233

Learn to:

❖ Give people the best of yourself
❖ Speak to be heard and speak to be felt
❖ Practice your conversation skills everyday
❖ Compliment strangers whenever possible

29

Honey Bees

When you've got good news spread it around

IT'S THE FIRST DAY OF SPRING and from the comfort of my porch I'm watching a squadron of honeybees flitting amongst the white clover on the front lawn.

The Egyptians, Greeks and Romans all revered bees and for good reason. Honey has been used as a food preservative, a sweetening agent, and an antiseptic for a long, long time. As well as feeding their hive colonies bees pollinate many fruits and vegetables. If honeybees went on strike and gave up their day jobs our kitchens would be missing one-third of all the foods we eat. And consider the flying hours they clock up. One bee has to make 154 trips to flowers to produce that teaspoon of honey we spread on our morning slice of toast.

However, my favorite part of the bee story is what happens after they return to base with their little saddlebags full of pollen crumbs.

After touching down the honeybee makes a beeline for the hive's main chamber. In the centre of the chamber is a dance floor. The bee shuffles on to it and begins tentatively tapping one foot. Heads turn. Encouraged it launches into its routine. It shimmies and jitterbugs its way up the dance floor, cuts to the left and semicircles back to the starting point – choreography that tells everyone the direction and distance of the flowers from the hive. The bee's excitement is infectious and pretty soon the dance floor is packed and line-dancing is in full swing. Every bee in the chamber is jiving, twisting and boot-scootin' to the same routine. After several circuits of the dance floor there is a sudden mad scramble for the exits as everyone heads off in search of the juicy flowers. This is Saturday night honeycomb fever at its very best. When bees want to share their good fortune they really do make a song and dance of it.

And it's not just the bees who have all the fun. When we enjoy our first baby steps it isn't long before our house is overrun by relatives keen to see the little moonwalker in action. Then we're off to primary school where one day our name is called out at assembly and we're awarded a certificate in front of the entire school. We can't get home fast enough to share the monumental news with our family. Years pass, we grow up, and out of the blue romantic love knocks at our door. Deliriously happy and feeling like the luckiest person in the world we enthrall our friends with a heartbeat by heartbeat description of our good fortune. And later we get to talk about our wedding. And our first child. And on and on it goes.

We're talking about one of the most powerful elixirs going around – *good news*. Sweeter to the ear than any nectar, more nourishing to the soul than any royal jelly, it's guaranteed to raise our spirits, strengthen our friendships, restore our faith in happy endings, and renew our motivation in striving for our personal dreams. When we deliver or receive good news we get all that and more. Best of all, it's free and it's ours any time we choose.

So, when you hear good news be sure to spread it around. Scream it from the rooftops and let others see you dancing a jig. The bees in their grooving discotheque know just how catching it can be.

Practice Happiness 29
Go to page 236

Learn to:

❖   Listen for good news, not bad news
❖   Avoid spreading bad news
❖   Spread good news everyday
❖   Encourage others to offer good news

30

Hitman

Look for opportunities to help people every day

GUARDIAN ANGELS COME IN MANY GUISES. They can be any age, any nationality, and can wear any manner of clothes. I know because I met mine in China and he dressed like a hitman.

Several years ago I made the surprising discovery that one of my great grandmothers was half Chinese. From that point on I felt a yearning to know more about the Chinese side of my heritage. So I took myself off to the land of the dragon and spent four weeks traipsing around the countryside from Beijing in the north to Lhasa in the south immersing myself in all the local customs and cuisines.

Two weeks into my trip and I was enjoying some down time in Nantong, a sleepy city on the northern banks of the Yangtze River. One day, shortly after finishing a light lunch of spring rolls and white wine, I found myself head down and backside up in a public toilet. This didn't feel like your usual bout of food poisoning. Thirty minutes later I staggered outside physically spent and five kilograms lighter. Only to be confronted by a man in black with dark wraparound sunglasses.

"You're sick." It wasn't a question. "Where does body hurt?"

He exuded authority and I was in no condition to argue. I told him that there was a pressure in my stomach and it felt like a knife had been plunged into the middle of my back. The pain was terrific.

He nodded and in fractured English said, "I am Mr. Wang. We go to hospital now."

After a hair-raising ride on the back of his motorbike through car-choked streets and rubbish-littered alleyways we arrived at a small clinic. Following a rapid-fire exchange in Mandarin with a group of nurses who regarded me with growing curiosity, Mr. Wang explained my options.

"They want to look at stomach Mr. Bruce," he said. "Three choices. Most expensive choice 330 Yuan. A thin lead with small light is put down throat."

"Sounds awful," I whined. "Other choices?"

"Second choice 250 Yuan. Very painful. They stick garden hose down throat with bigger light."

I swallowed nervously. "Last choice?"

"Only 150 Yuan. Very cheap. Doctor sticks hands down throat, one holding torch, other hand holding Canon camera," he said with a cheeky grin.

"Let's go with the first choice," I quickly replied.

I was ushered into a room with a doctor and three nurses who fussed all over me. None spoke a word of English. To allay my obvious apprehension Mr. Wang kept up a running commentary of the procedure. After being directed to lie on a table on my left side the doctor inserted a long thin black lead with a microscopic light and camera at the tip into my right nostril which was slowly fed down my throat and into my stomach. Without a doubt the weirdest sensation I have ever experienced. Whenever I opened my eyes Mr. Wang, my guardian angel in black, was there watching over me, offering nods of encouragement.

The pictures taken of my stomach revealed a tear in my duodenum in the small intestine, a stomach ulcer. The doctor gave me a pill which provided immediate relief. Then a lively conversation between the doctor and my guardian angel – actually more haggling than conversation – concluded that medication, and not surgery, would be sufficient treatment.

"Medicine will fix your stomach," Mr. Wang told me with some gravity. "But you must have three meals every day at same time. And no more baijiu (*local white wine with 60% alcohol content*). No more alcohol. You MUST look after stomach Mr. Bruce." The sincerity of his words had me nodding my head furiously.

Mr. Wang took me to a nearby pharmacy to have my prescription filled and then we shared a pot of Chinese tea at a small restaurant.

"Mr. Wang, thank you so much for your help today. I don't know how I would have managed without you. Is....is there any way I can repay your kindness?"

"Helping Mr. Bruce is payment enough. I help you today, tomorrow you help another. And now I must go to work."

And after a formal bow of his head he hopped on his motorbike, reminded me once last time to look after my stomach, and was gone. He never did take off his sunglasses. My very own hitman guardian angel.

You and I are surrounded by guardian angels. We see them performing selfless and good-spirited acts every day: the schoolboy who gives his seat to the elderly lady on the morning train; the person who compliments a stranger on their colorful dress; the driver who pulls over on the highway to check whether the owner of the car with the flat tire needs help; the girl who readily pays another shopper's shortfall at the cashier; the office worker who openly encourages other employees; the lady who looks for another motorist to give her unused parking ticket to; the woman who gives a cold bottle of water to a bus driver on a hot summers day; the person in the city who walks a lost tourist to her destination; the gentleman who gives a warm greeting to a passer-by on the street.

They're guardian angels, each and every one of them. They're looking for opportunities to make someone else's load a little bit lighter. And in the process they're helping to develop a kinder, more connected community.

So, when you get the chance to be a guardian angel seize it wholeheartedly with both wings. And when someone helps you remember to repay their act of kindness by paying it forward. Like Mr. Wang.

As a Chinese proverb says:
If you want happiness for an hour take a nap;
If you want happiness for a day – go fishing;
If you want happiness for a year – inherit a fortune;
If you want happiness for a lifetime – help someone else.

Practice Happiness 30
Go to page 239

Learn to:
❖ Practice daily random acts of kindness
❖ Be a cheer squad for others
❖ Surprise your loved ones each week

31

Trash and Treasure Market

We are all very similar and all very different

TREASURE ISLAND WAS THE MOST POPULAR BOOK when I was in grade three. Compulsory reading for all. Playtimes saw hordes of shrieking Blackbeards and Long John Silvers tearing around the playground trailing Jolly Roger flags and brandishing cardboard cutlasses. No favor was given and walking the plank was common, an indignity I suffered most days being guilty of being short for my age. For all our efforts we never did find any gold buried behind the tuck shop or dusty treasure maps on the shelves of the library.

But the hunt for treasure continues. And let me tell you that sometimes "X" does indeed mark the spot – especially when you are using a GPS that leads you directly to the Camberwell Trash and Treasure Market.

Every Sunday morning a car park as large as a football field transforms into a maze of stalls full of bustling crowds, hawking vendors, and music buskers.

Most people come to the market for the same reason. They're here to rummage through mountains of second-hand jetsam and flotsam in the hope of a bargain and to save themselves a quid. A set of old crockery to help get started in a new flat, a pair of used-Levi's to save spending money for a new pair, an old lawn mower to replace the broken mower in the shed, a shoebox of assorted toys to serve as Christmas presents for the kids.

Another group of people look at all the junk in a completely different way. I call them the mental alchemists. My sister is one of these people. Instead of seeing what is, they see what could be. They see potential. The mental alchemists are remarkably creative and innovative. Bent cutlery is turned into a set of wind chimes. Watering cans and worn out gum boots become flowerpots. A lone oar is recycled as a curtain rod. A ship's porthole is restored as a mirror frame. An old wringer washing machine finds new life as a beer cooler.

And everyone, mental alchemist or not, has their own unique story to tell about what an item means to them. A couple of badly scratched 7-inch vinyl singles – "*California Dreamin*" by The Mamas and the Papas, and Buffalo Springfield's "*There's Something Happening Here*" – wouldn't exactly have me fumbling for my wallet. But for the hippie vendor, these were the anthems of the anti-Vietnam War demonstrations that he marched along to back in '69. A mass-produced framed picture of Doris Day would be meaningless to many. But not to the vendor whose recently deceased wife had been a lifelong fan and had travelled all the way to America to have the picture signed by the great woman herself. And a battered and bruised Six Million Dollar Man action figure doll capable of running faster and seeing further, and able to beat the crap out of other action figures might seem like junk to others. But to me it would bring back fond memories of the nights my father and I watched the TV series together in the '70s.

After a morning of browsing countless stalls and hearing many such stories you'd be forgiven for thinking that we are more different than we are alike.

And yet – have you noticed that retro is the *new* cool? Skinny jeans and sunglasses that cover half your face are back in. As are fedoras and hot pants. And glamour wave hairstyles for women and slicked back tapers for men. And yo-yos and scooters and Rubik's Cubes for children. Every few years the old fashions, hairstyles and toys keep making a comeback. And where are the younger crowd going to stock up on this stuff? Trash and treasure markets, of course. Maybe, the young people of today have more in common with their parents and grandparents than they care to admit.

This is why I love going to the markets. They testify to the wonderful diversity and similarity of people everywhere. Even though we might often think about things differently, we are more alike than we realize. Despite our varying ages and different backgrounds the stories from the market remind me that we all share the same basic needs. We all want to belong, to realize our ambitions, to love and be loved, and to be happy. And yes, sometimes we want to wear the same clothes too.

If you visit the market, look out for me. You'll spot me easily enough. I'll be the guy trading stories with the owner of a stuffed rooster or trying on a pair of WWII pilot's goggles.

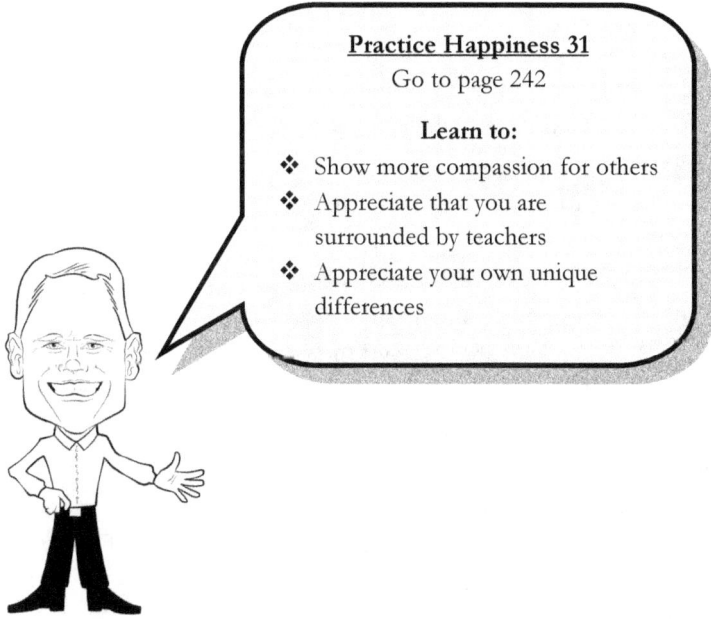

Practice Happiness 31
Go to page 242

Learn to:
❖ Show more compassion for others
❖ Appreciate that you are surrounded by teachers
❖ Appreciate your own unique differences

32

Pet Beagle

Focus on understanding the other person first

MY BEAGLE'S NAME IS CLANCY. Solidly built like a Hummer, an orange coat with white socks, and a perpetual mischievous grin. A muscled ball of non-stop riotous energy.

After two years I understand him pretty well. When he's happy his ears become motorbike handles and he lets out a soft chuckle and when he's been caught chewing laces or eating remotes he drops his head, purses his lips like he's sucking on a straw, and slowly shakes his muzzle from side to side as if to say, "I tell you, it wasn't my fault. The voices told me to do it."

But when I first got him some of Clancy's behaviors left me slightly flummoxed. Most memorable were the times he went through his Jekyll and Hyde routine. It was always on a Sunday afternoon. He went from a beagle into a werewolf. Hunched back, stiffened limbs, distended paws, narrowed eyes, a snarling rictus. In a word, frightening.

From Clancy's perspective, I can only guess what he was thinking.

"What's wrong with you humans? I've had experience with this monster and let me tell you that it's only going to cause you pain and misery. I mean, just look at the thing. It doesn't have any fur or legs or even a face, just a bloated red belly and an incredibly long skinny neck with a mean, toothless mouth.

And why release it from its cage in the first place? Grabbing it by the scruff of the neck, tying it to a wall and then poking its backside obviously annoys the heck out of the thing. But in every room *you keep on doing it*. And that ghastly wail as it tries to swallow everything in sight. Terrifying. I hope you realize the efforts I make to try and distract it so you can all make a run for it.

And after 20 minutes of screaming humans and slamming doors and total madness you give the beast another poke on its backside, it lets out a drawn-out sigh, and promptly falls fast asleep. What gives? Then you drag it back to its lair giving it another week to work out how to eat us all. What am I missing here? I tell you, *if the thing catches you, you won't be able to sit down for a week!"*

Did you guess Clancy's nemesis? That's right – the vacuum cleaner. At first we just attributed his behavior to game-playing antics. But when he started exhibiting signs of extreme stress and irritability we decided it was high time to approach the local vet. The vet knew Clancy's history and told us that he had been abused by his previous owner, who when drunk would go into fits of rage and hit Clancy with a stick. The penny dropped. A long handle connected to a noisy vacuum cleaner probably seemed like an angry man wielding a stick in Clancy's eyes.

But how could we have been expected to know what Clancy was thinking and feeling whenever he saw the vacuum cleaner? I'm no Doctor Doolittle. I don't understand doggie-speak. I didn't know his background, the experiences he had had before coming into my home.

Pretty silly, right? Well, it's just as silly for us to expect to know what *another person* is thinking in a particular situation. Just because we've all got arms and legs and walk upright doesn't mean we all think the same. Not by a long shot. Remember that a person's thoughts and beliefs, shaped by a lifetime of family and social and cultural experiences, are unique to each individual.

Maybe when you mentioned a shopping expedition to a friend, you were thinking shopping on the cheap at Walmart and Target stores, while they were anticipating maxing out the credit card at more exclusive boutique shops. Maybe when you planned meeting someone for coffee at 9 o'clock, you were thinking 9AM, while they thought you meant 9PM (don't laugh, this happened to me more than once in Saudi Arabia where they are predominantly a nighttime culture).

We get into the habit of expecting others to be thinking the same thoughts as ourselves at a particular moment. This results in a lot of our arguments. Particularly in relationships. After our partner experiences a certain situation we think to ourselves, "That's the same situation I faced. Therefore, I know exactly how she is feeling and I know why she behaved that way." Which usually brings the well-worn response, "How do you know what I'm thinking? You have *no idea* how I'm feeling." And the argument escalates from there.

The key to avoiding these misunderstandings is being able to understand the other person's world. To see the world from *their* perspective. Instead of trying to *guess* or assume what the other person is thinking and feeling you want to *know* what they are thinking and feeling. You achieve this by listening to them and by asking them questions to discover what's important to them and why they feel the way they do. You set aside your own need to talk and to be understood and put your entire focus into understanding the other person.

There are several wonderful benefits in doing this. The other person will recognize and appreciate that you put your respect for them and their position above your own position. Consequently, any disagreements are likely to be resolved much more quickly as each person becomes less concerned about who is right or wrong, and more concerned with respecting each other. And, by listening to the other person without expectations or judgments your mind will be open to new ideas and discoveries. Also, by truly listening to each other you will be able to connect more meaningfully at a much deeper level, the main ingredient in healthier, more loving relationships.

I think we can learn a lot from our pets when it comes to understanding others. Just like us, everything they do they do for a reason. If we wish to understand that reason all we need to do is watch them and listen to them. It's the same with people.

And Clancy is a lot happier now. He's always left outside now with a yummy bone when the monster is released from its lair.

<u>Practice Happiness 32</u>
Go to page 245

Learn to:
❖ Ask more open-ended questions when involved in a misunderstanding
❖ Clear your mind of judgments, expectations, and assumptions
❖ Look for the element of truth in the other person's words

33

Computer Newbie

Look for the positive intention behind a person's behavior

THE FIRST TIME I SAT DOWN AT A COMPUTER was in August of 1994. It was in an old storage room in the university library that had been converted into a computer lab. Some two dozen Apple computers sat on rows of desks. It was cramped and it was noisy. Fingers chicken-pecked at keyboards with the sound of ravenous chipmunks and a solitary printer in the corner buzz sawed without rest.

And there was I. Three months out from having to submit my PhD dissertation and I hadn't typed a word. Sure, I'd *written* a few. Five hundred pages in fact, but it was all squiggles and hieroglyphs. The time had arrived to start typing. At a computer. I was terrified.

In front of me sat a Macintosh Classic II. It resembled a miniature World War II bunker, squat with an air of indestructibility, a little porthole near its base. I stared at it with apprehension. How to start it? Mmmm.

I stared at the keyboard. There were no buttons or switches. Nothing that said "Start" or "On". I took a big breath......relaaaxxxx. Trying not to advertise my ignorance I let my hands casually wander over the sides of the computer's casing while glancing out of the corner of my eye at the student beside me. My fingers poked, probed, fiddled.

DONG. I flicked a switch on the rear left side of the casing and was rewarded with a start-up chime and a greeting "Welcome to Macintosh" on the monitor. I sat back feeling well pleased with myself and even managed a smile at the student beside me who smiled back.

I had heard on the grapevine that to see any action on the computer's monitor one had to operate a palm-sized device called a mouse. Which was connected to the keyboard via a cord. After a bit of experimenting I found that by moving the mouse I was able to maneuver a little arrowhead around the screen. When the arrowhead was at the top of the screen I clicked on the front left part of the mouse with my index finger and – voila – a drop-down menu of programs appeared. Around and around the screen I went. Moving and clicking on all the programs. I was off to a flying start.

And then….disaster.

No matter where I moved the mouse I couldn't seem to maneuver the arrowhead past a certain point on the far right side of the screen. The mouse cord just didn't seem to be long enough. I looked carefully at the cord. No knots, no tangles. I leaned to my right and stretched the cord to its very limit. Didn't help. I took a big breath……relaaaxxxx. The student to my right looked at me and smiled. I smiled back through clenched teeth.

I tried moving the keyboard to the right reasoning that as the cord was attached to the keyboard, and the keyboard was connected to the computer, it might move the arrowhead to the right. But all this did was bring me on a collision course with the keyboard of the student on my right. He looked at me again, this time with a grin.

"Maybe I can help you," he said.

"Thanks, but I don't see how," I replied. "I think I need to find another computer."

"Let me guess. You can't move the arrowhead pointer on the screen?"

My eyes widened in surprise. "Wow, how did you know?"

"I guessed as much when I saw you stretching the mouse cord. I had already penned you for a newbie after watching you hunting for the power switch. But moving the keyboard just now – *that* was a classic."

We both laughed. He showed me how to move the arrowhead pointer – a little ball beneath the mouse. Lift the mouse, roll the ball and you move the pointer anywhere you want.

I tried it with instant success. "Thanks. Good thing you were here or I might have killed the mouse in frustration."

"I've found that there's always a good reason why people do things…..even things that seem a bit weird, like torturing a computer mouse."

You find enlightened souls in the most unexpected places. And I know what he means. Like those times when you see people doing things that seem so *obviously wrong*. Like the guy in the gym slinging free weights around in a dangerous-looking fashion. Or the mother in the park yelling at her child. Or the person continuing to smoke in spite of all the health warnings. Or the motorist dodging erratically from lane to lane on a congested freeway. I even catch myself driving down dead-end streets from time to time.

However, as my wise computer mentor said, every person does what they do for a good reason. We may not know the reason, we may not even understand the reason, but to the individual their behavior is serving a specific purpose. In other words, every behavior is motivated by a positive intention.

The fellow in the gym may actually believe he is lifting weights using the correct technique. The mother may have just stopped her young boy from chasing his ball across the road. The erratic driver may be racing to the hospital after receiving news that his wife collapsed at work. And I keep thinking that zooming down dead-end streets is going to save me driving time…..but it never does.

The point is that once we understand that everyone behaves the way they do for a good reason – a reason that makes sense to them given their needs and their current resources – it compels us to give them the benefit of the doubt. Isn't this exactly what we do with our friends and loved ones anyway? We avoid pre-judging them, and instead choose to believe the best about them.

(By the way, giving people the benefit of the doubt doesn't mean that we condone everyone's actions. Once a person's positive intention is recognized, alternative behaviors that are less harmful and more appropriate for a situation can be suggested, for example, exercising as a healthier way to relieve stress than smoking.)

When we give people the benefit of the doubt it allows the best in ourselves to shine brighter. We learn to be more compassionate. We are more tolerant of others, more respectful, and more trusting. We become less critical and judgmental, less susceptible to negativity. We are less stressed. We are more content.

And then the magic happens. Because we are no longer focused on finding reasons to criticize or condemn people for their behavior, we start looking for and seeing *the best in others*. Instead of only seeing another's faults and shortcomings, we begin focusing on a person's good qualities. We become more accepting of other people's differences. Suddenly the world seems a much friendlier place where we see every stranger as a potential friend.

It all starts when we give each other the benefit of the doubt.

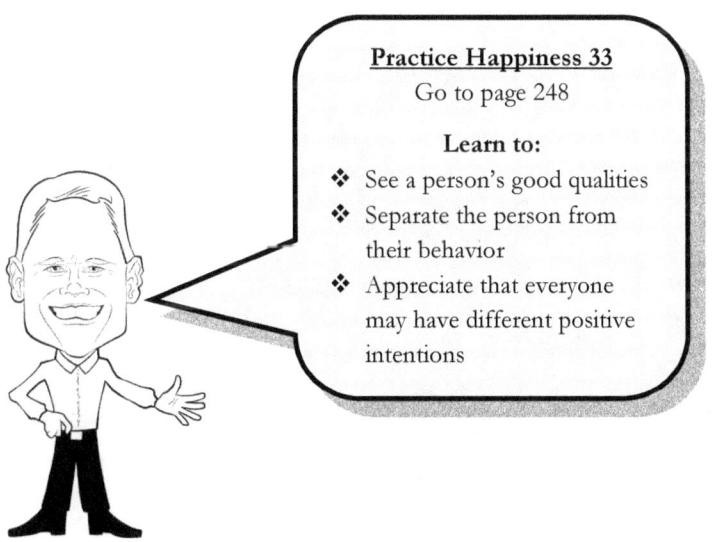

Practice Happiness 33
Go to page 248

Learn to:
❖ See a person's good qualities
❖ Separate the person from their behavior
❖ Appreciate that everyone may have different positive intentions

PART TWO

Practice
Happiness

Step

1

Live from the Inside Out

Be the person you are meant to be

In this step

You are responsible for your happiness and unhappiness

*

The way you think determines your feelings

*

It is always your choice how you react to a situation

*

Avoid playing The Excuses Game

*

Recognize your strengths and ignite your passion

*

Live your values for greater contentment

*

Avoid comparing yourself to others

*

Accept that there are no mistakes, only results

*

Be your own best friend

*

Find a charitable cause that interests you

*

Identify a job you are passionate about

*

Define your life purpose

Practice Happiness 1

Your feelings of happiness are your own responsibility

Learn to:

❖ Change your feelings by changing your thoughts
❖ Reduce your stress by changing your thoughts
❖ Appreciate the role of controllability in happiness
❖ Accept your role in your own unhappiness

---

1. Become aware of your feelings and thoughts

Self-awareness is the first and most important step in pursuing greater happiness. Start keeping a Feelings Diary (see Table 1). In it regularly record your feelings, the type of situation you experienced, your physical symptoms, the likely automatic thought that would have elicited the associated feeling and physical symptom, and positive alternative interpretations of any negative automatic thoughts. Several examples have been provided.

Feelings	Physical symptoms	Situation	Automatic thought	Alternative thought
Excitement	Energized	Preparing to go on a run	I'm looking forward to this run	
Bored	Sloth like	Shopping with the wife	What a waste of time!	This is my chance to develop some compassion
Disappointment	Hollow emptiness	The boss criticized my project	I'm hopeless	I'll learn from this experience
Tense	Fast shallow breathing	Stuck in traffic jam	Oh, great! Just my luck!	I can't do anything, I might as well relax or plan ahead
Sadness	Biting fingernails	A friend ignored me	Why is she angry with me?	Maybe she's preoccupied with her own issues

Table 1

2. Notice that your thoughts drive your feelings

As you continue keeping your Feelings Diary, keep an eye out for patterns. Over time you will start noticing that you have particular types of thoughts when you are feeling various emotions. For example, feelings of happiness and excitement might be associated with certain positive thoughts (e.g. "Boy, I'm looking forward to this run", "I'm really pleased with the work I did on that project); while feelings of despondency and sadness might be associated with a negative thought (e.g. "I'm dreading going on this run", "I'm so disappointed with my project").

3. Decrease your stress by changing your thoughts

Your Feelings Diary clearly illustrates the powerful influence of your thoughts in determining your feelings. So the next time you feel stressed identify the nature of your automatic thought (it will invariably be negative putdown language) and replace it with an optimistic upbeat alternative thought. Many strategies for managing your emotions will be described throughout this Practice Happiness section of the book but this will always remain your first and most powerful strategy.

4. Understand controllability – your happiness depends upon it!

Being able to distinguish between those situations you can control and those you cannot control will save you a lot of needless stress and unhappiness. For example, you have a degree of control in whether to resign from a job, leave a relationship, help a stranger on the street, plan for the future, or step out of a long queue. On the other hand, you have NO control over the rain, traffic jams, the stock market, the past, or whether your girlfriend will return your feelings. Also, you have NO control over another person's feelings. They are responsible for their own happiness. So, *don't let things outside of your control dictate your happiness.* Focus your energies solely on the situations you can influence as well as the way that you react mentally, emotionally, and physically to events.

List some of the occasions (and people) you encounter during your day that you have no control over.

_____

_____

5. Accept that you alone are responsible for your own feelings

Your Feelings Diary will have helped you realize that you, and you alone, are responsible for your feelings – the good ones and the bad ones. From now on, when you want to have more happy feelings realize that the first step involves you making the conscious choice to have more positive thoughts. Looking back at your Diary will remind you to replace any negative automatic thoughts with more optimistic thoughts.

6. Accept that you will need to make changes in your life to be happier

Choosing to be happier usually requires having to make changes to one's life – we've already spoken about changing some of your thoughts – but other changes may be necessary too. Changes such as the type of friends you keep, your choice of activities, developing better ways to communicate with your spouse, practicing more gratitude and compassion. Happiness doesn't happen by accident. You must consciously choose to be happy and then take action to make it happen.

Put on your favorite happy song (mine is "Staying Alive" by the Bee Gees). Dance on the spot like there's no tomorrow. Why? Because it's fun! And it will make you feel instantly happy!

7. Stop expecting others to be responsible for your happiness

Reflect upon those occasions in your life when you find yourself thinking or saying aloud that other people are responsible for your happiness (e.g. when a friend declines your invitation for a dinner outing – "You have made me so unhappy!", when your partner fails to respond to your amorous advances – "Darling, don't you want to make me happy?"). List some of those times.

_____

_____

Your own thoughts determine your feelings. Control your thoughts, control your feelings.

8. Take responsibility for your own unhappiness

Consider the example of a relationship breakup. Afterwards you can choose to be happy or you can choose to be bitter and harbor feelings of resentment. If you choose to be happy you must practice forgiveness. You must forgive the other person and you must forgive yourself. Accept that each party has their own cross to bear and that life is too short to be bottled up with resentment and anger. Above all else, love yourself and fill your heart with peace and happiness. There isn't room in your heart for love and hate. Choose to let go of feelings of unhappiness.

Think of a specific situation in which you are unhappy (e.g. relationship breakup, argument with a work colleague, parking ticket, job salary). How is it serving you by remaining unhappy?

_____

_____

What will be the benefits of letting go of your unhappiness?

_____

_____

What MUST you do (e.g. forgive the person or yourself, clarify the situation by speaking to the person, focus on the silver lining) to move forwards?

_____

_____

Extra Resources

McKay, M., Davis, M., & Fanning, P. (2011). *Thoughts and feelings: Taking control of your mood and life.* Oakland, Canada: New Harbinger Publications.

Practice Happiness 2

Be prepared to take responsibility for your circumstances

Learn to:

❖ Recognize the role you play in your successes and disappointments

❖ Stop making excuses

❖ Accept that it is your choice how you react

❖ See every situation as a learning experience

❖ Forgive yourself so you can move forward

---

1. Be prepared to take responsibility for the results in your life

Think back over the triumphs and successes you've experienced in your life. Straight away write down 5 of the most memorable. Also write down the role you played in making them happen.

_____

_____

Now write down 5 of your most memorable disappointments. Again, write down the role you played in making them happen.

_____

_____

You may have found it difficult to think of your most memorable disappointments. And you may have been tempted to attribute the outcome to bad luck or the actions of others. We can be quick to claim the credit for successes in our life but slow in accepting responsibility for our mistakes or setbacks. But if you are ever to become the true master and commander of your ship you need to take ownership of ALL the results you experience, the good and the bad.

2. Be prepared to identify and own your own excuses

Do you sometimes make excuses, blame others, or avoid taking responsibility for your actions? When we make excuses for the results in our life we give away control of our actions as well as any chance we have to improve our actions in the future. We take our self from the playing court and confine our self to the spectator stands. Consider keeping a notepad with you at all times to record your excuses.

Over the past 2 days what (if any) excuses did you make at work, at home? Think hard. Describe the situations and the excuses.

_____

_____

Once you learn to recognize your excuses you can begin to stop making them and start taking greater control of your life.

3. Be prepared to accept that it is your choice how you react

The keystone principle underlying all personal development programs is that every individual can choose how they respond to any situation. No matter how dire the circumstances – losing your job, being involved in a car accident or getting divorced – you have control over how you react. It's your choice. You can choose to see the situation as a learning experience from which you will grow and be wiser down the road or you can clench your fists, play the victim role, and become embroiled in a whirlpool of negative emotions. Accept that there are *always* choices.

List 5 difficult situations you faced recently in your life and describe how you chose to react. Did you react in a positive or a negative way?

_____

_____

4. Be prepared to ask yourself: "What part did I play in this outcome?"

This can be a bit bruising on the ego but it represents the most important step in adopting a full-responsibility attitude to the circumstances in your life. Whenever something happens in your life ask this question. Example situations may include: being caught speeding, missing out on a promotion, having an argument with your partner, a colleague ignoring you at work, becoming overweight, being unsuccessful on an e-dating website, having friends rarely ask you out. Always assume that you contributed *somehow* to the situation. Dig deep for the answers. By continuing to blame others you condemn yourself to repeating the same mistakes again and again. However, by acknowledging your role you give yourself the opportunity to improve or change a part of yourself.

5. Be prepared to ask yourself: "What can I learn from this experience?"

This is an exciting step because now you get to learn from your mistakes. Viewing every situation you encounter as a potential learning experience will greatly increase your confidence in yourself at solving problems. The result – less confusion, less anxiety, and greater happiness.

6. Be prepared to ask yourself: "Which response is consistent with my goals and values?"

When you are unsure of which choice to make in a particular situation re-examine your goals and values. Which response would take me a step closer towards my goals? Which response would be in harmony with my values (e.g. health, security, love, integrity)? Whichever response you choose you will be exercising more responsibility and gleaning the benefits of taking greater control of your life.

7. Be prepared to consider what taking full responsibility will look like?

Imagine a day in your life when you never make excuses or play the blame game. How might you respond differently to your partner if they accused you of doing no housework? Instead of fumbling with excuses which only serve to disempower you and diminish your standing in the eyes of your partner, ask yourself the questions from the three previous activities. Table 2 will give you the opportunity to practice these questions using your own circumstances. Two examples have been provided for you.

Circumstance	Excuse	Goals and values	What part did I play in this outcome?	What can I learn from this experience?
An accident driving my car	Car in front braked too quickly; car in front was driving too slowly; driver was an elderly man (wearing a hat)	Driving responsibly and being a safe driver	I may have been too close to the car in front of me; I wasn't paying close enough attention; I was talking to my passenger	Leave more room between my car and other cars; concentrate on driving; drive slower
Argument with wife about my not doing enough housework	I was too tired; the kids should be doing more housework duties; I was too busy	Wanting a strong loving relationship based upon equality and mutual respect with my wife	I was too selfish; I wanted to watch the football on TV; I worked hard all day (so did she but that's beside the point)	Don't take my partner for granted; be more compassionate; think about the day she may have had

Table 2

8. Be prepared to forgive yourself and move forward

A key part of assuming total responsibility is being able to forgive ourselves and others for mistakes. No one is perfect; toss that disempowering expectation out the window straight away. Pursuing your goals and your life purpose means that you can expect to make mistakes, and lots of them. The more mistakes, the more learning opportunities, the greater self-growth. Be kind to yourself. Be your own best fan. Be proud of yourself for having the courage to follow your dreams.

Challenge yourself to make zero excuses for a whole week. If you make a mistake take responsibility straight away. (Have fun watching the surprised reaction on other people's faces.) Notice how your feelings of indecision and anxiety dissolve. Learn from the experience. And forgive yourself.

Extra Resources

Izzo, J. B. (2012). *Stepping up: How taking responsibility changes everything.* San Francisco, CA: Berrett-Koehler Publishers.

Practice Happiness 3
Recognize your strengths and ignite your passion

Learn to:

❖ Identify your strengths
❖ Make the greatest use of your strengths
❖ Persevere with your strengths
❖ Avoid listening to others' expectations of you

---

1. Identify your strengths

There are 3 common methods for identifying one's strengths.

(a) The first method is called the Self-Portrait Method. It is a subjective method where you write down your answers to the following questions to create a self-portrait of whom you are and when you are at your best.

What things were you good at doing as a child?

_____

_____

What things are you passionate about?

_____

_____

What things give you energy and feelings of vitality?

_____

_____

What things do you do where your learning seems rapid and enjoyable?

_____

_____

What things do you do well and almost effortlessly?

_____

_____

What things make you feel alive and fulfilled?

_____

_____

What activities make you lose track of time?

_____

_____

What things do people typically ask you for help with?

_____

_____

(b) The second method is called the Reflected Best Self Exercise.

Email about a dozen people who know you well and ask them to write an account of a time when you were at your best. Then using the common patterns from the responses create a portrait of your strengths.

(c) The final method is called Gallup's StrengthsFinder. It is another subjective method and requires you to answer a number of self-assessment questions.

2. How to maximize use of your strengths
Having identified your strengths now you need to ensure that you are doing everything you can to make the best use of them.

(a) First, you need to devote time to improve your strengths. We're talking about regular practice over a number of years which will require constant sacrifices, discipline, attention to feedback, and many moments of boredom and frustration. Think of the long hours elite athletes and concert musicians dedicate to mastering their craft. And so will you.

What are some small things you could be doing on a daily or weekly basis to improve your strengths?

_____

_____

(b) Second, you need to start using your strengths in as many situations as possible, for example, work and non-work environments. This will give you more opportunities to develop your strengths and become comfortable using them. For example, one of my strengths is public speaking so every chance I get I speak at schools, at Wellness fairs, at Rotary clubs, at libraries.

In what other environments could you be using your strengths?

_____

_____

(c) Third, you need to construct a personal development plan to ensure that you are constantly developing and improving your strengths. Example plan activities might include ongoing courses, working with a coach or mentor, attending workshops, or gaining advice from other experts in your field.

What are 5 things you could plan to do over the next 3 months to improve your strengths?

_____

_____

3. Ignore other people's expectations of you

Don't let yourself become distracted by the negativity or conformist attitudes and prejudices of others. And be careful not to compare yourself with others. Just as Susan Boyle did, focus on the unique flavor you will add to your strength. It is your signature difference that will allow you to stand out from the crowd and succeed. Remain focused on your supporters who expect you to succeed.

Design a placard with a photo of you performing your strength. Under the photo write the key behaviors and thoughts associated with you performing your strength. Make multiple copies of this motivational placard and place it in prominent places around your home, in your car, and at your office.

You may find yourself tempted to succumb to the hard work and constant discipline necessary to develop your strengths. You must resist falling back into your old ways of doing things. These 5 tips will help you persevere with your strengths.

- Keep reminding yourself of your values and make sure you live those values each and every day.
- Every day visualize yourself successfully having mastered your strengths and achieving your goal.
- Surround yourself with people who believe in you and your goal.
- Acknowledge all of your progress steps, no matter how small. This will help you remain motivated and sustain your own belief in your ability to reach your goal.
- Regularly reward yourself for your efforts.

Extra Resources

Buckingham, M., & Clifton, D. O. (2001). *Now, discover your strengths.* New York, NY: The Free Press.

Rath, T. (2007). *StrengthsFinder 2.0.* New York, NY: The Free Press.

Practice Happiness 4

Trusting in your values will keep you on course

Learn to:

❖ Identify your values

❖ Be happier by living your values

❖ Make more effective decisions by aligning your values with your actions

❖ Trust in your values

---

1. Identify your values

You are going to identify your values so that you have a clear understanding of the things you value most in life. Living a life true to your values will ensure that you are living authentically and being true to yourself. Which means you will be a whole lot happier! Later we will talk about how you go about living your values but for now we need to begin by identifying your values.

(a) Start by recalling those moments in your life when you felt happiest. Think about the factors that made you feel so happy – what you were doing, where you were, the people you were with, the time of the year.

_____

_____

Now identify those times when you felt most fulfilled and satisfied. Once again, think about the factors that contributed to these feelings.

_____

_____

From your answers you want to arrive at a list of your most important 20 values. You should feel a real sense of passion or excitement about these words. To help you I have listed some common values below. For more comprehensive lists of values google the descriptor "list of personal values" on the Internet.

Ability	Entertainment	Ingenuity
Acceptance	Enthusiasm	Intelligence
Achievement	Excellence	Intimacy
Adventure	Expertise	Introversion
Affection	Exploration	Inventiveness
Ambition	Extroversion	Justice
Artfulness	Facilitating	Kindness
Attentiveness	Fairness	Leadership
Balance	Faith	Learning
Belongingness	Fashion	Logic
Bravery	Finesse	Loyalty
Calmness	Fitness	Mindfulness
Carefulness	Flexibility	Motivation
Cheerfulness	Focus	Neatness
Clarity	Freedom	Open-mindedness
Commitment	Friendliness	Optimism
Compassion	Fun	Organization
Connection	Generosity	Passion
Cooperation	Genuineness	Peacefulness
Creativity	Giving	Perseverance
Decisiveness	Gratefulness	Playfulness
Dependability	Gregariousness	Popularity
Dexterity	Growth	Practicality

Diplomacy	Happiness	Precision
Direction	Health	Proactivity
Diversity	Honesty	Professionalism
Education	Hospitality	Punctuality
Efficiency	Humor	Realism
Empathy	Imagination	Refinement
Encouragement	Impact	Resilience
Endurance	Impartiality	Sensitivity
Energy	Independence	Variety
Enjoyment	Industriousness	Wealth

Now write down your top 20 values.

_____

_____

(b) Second, reduce your list of 20 values down to your most important 10 values.

_____

_____

(c) Third, rank your values from 1, most important, to 10, least important. If you find that you struggle to choose which of two values is more important imagine a scenario involving them. For example, if you cannot decide between Education and Fitness, ask the question, "On most occasions, if I had to choose, would I prefer to spend time reading and studying or having a workout?"

Write your final 10 ranked values here.

1.	_____	6.	_____
2.	_____	7.	_____
3.	_____	8.	_____
4.	_____	9.	_____
5.	_____	10.	_____

2. Being aware of your values and your feelings can help you make effective decisions

When you know your values you can use them to help you make key decisions. Whenever you are struggling with a decision (e.g. choosing between working longer hours and spending more time with family) choose one of your options and then listen to your feelings. Your feelings are a barometer of the alignment between your actions and your values. If you value hard work and financial security but you choose to spend more time with your family (and less time at work), there will be a conflict between your values and your actions. This will result in feelings of disharmony in your gut – that knotted feeling of having a tight ball in your stomach. Alternatively, when your actions are aligned with your values you are in harmony and you have feelings of fullness, contentment, happiness, and warmth.

What is a big decision you are wrestling with at the moment?

_____

_____

In your mind choose one of the possible options available to you. Fully imagine how your life would be if you followed through with that option. How would the amount of time you have at work and away from work change? Would you have more or less available money? Would having more or less money affect your life? How would your choice impact on your energy levels?

_____

_____

Now listen to your feelings having made that choice. Do you feel knotted feelings of disharmony or contentment feelings of harmony? If you experience feelings of disharmony weigh up your choice against each of your values. Is your choice aligned with your values? To attain feelings of harmony you will have to either change your choice (to reflect your values) or change your values. What did you ultimately decide to do?

_____

_____

3. How would you know if you were living your values?

Now it's time to road test your values and start living them fully. Let's look at an example. If being healthy is one of your key values what exactly should you be doing each day to express that value?

Look at the example in Table 3 below. Repeat the columns for several of your own most important values. You may discover that you need to change some of your behaviors, thought patterns, or physical states to better reflect your key values.

Value	Value-aligned behaviors	Value-aligned thoughts	Value-aligned physical state
Health	Regular exercise; healthy food choices; right amount of sleep; non-smoker; limited alcohol; daily flexibility exercises	Always confident of being able to complete physical tasks; proud of the way you care for your body	Usually feel full of energy; rarely feel any aches and pains; have sufficient energy for daily tasks; rarely get sick

Table 3

4. Are you spending *enough time* living your values?

This activity will help you pinpoint particular life areas in which you need to concentrate more of your energies if you are to more fully live your values. Consider your life consisting of the 8 areas in Figure 1 below.

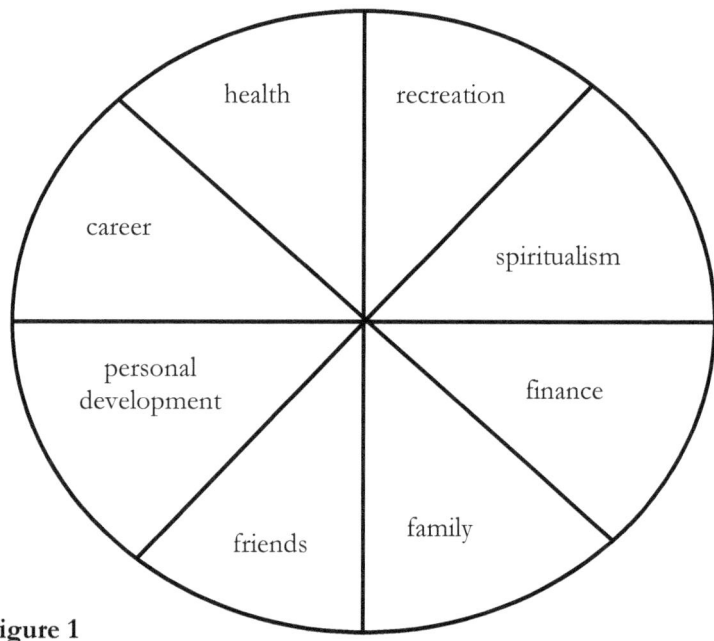

Figure 1

For each area how satisfied do you *presently feel?* Give yourself a score out of 10 (with 10 being totally satisfied) for each area.

Now give yourself a score out of 10 about how satisfied you *wish to feel* in each area.

Examine the discrepancy between your scores for each of the 8 life areas. Focus your attention on those life areas that are most reflective of your key values. Maybe finance is very important to you. Let's pretend you scored 7 for your present satisfaction level for 'finance', while you wish to score 9 in the future. Now you can think about what new behaviors, thoughts, and physical states you will need to introduce into your daily or weekly schedule to get that 7 up to a 9. Do the same thing for the other life areas that are most important to you.

Have your partner do this activity as well. Examining each other's scores can be incredibly enlightening. You will understand a lot more about each other's perceptions and actual behaviors.

5. Seek the observations of those closest to you

Sometimes we can become blind to our own behaviors. So ask family members or close friends whether they see you living your values. Ask them for specific examples.

6. Putting it all together and *trusting* in your values

Once you are practicing all of the previous activities you will increasingly become more in tune with personal feelings of harmony and disharmony, the signals that tell you whether you are living according to your values or not. Trusting in your values will gradually gain in strength following your successful attempts at making your daily behaviors better reflect your values. So, make sure you acknowledge all of your successes, always reward yourself, and commit yourself fully to your goals confident in the knowledge that you are following a course true to your authentic self.

Extra Resources

Harris, R. (2008). *The happiness trap: How to stop struggling and start living.* Boston, MASS: Trumpeter Books.

Smith, H. W. (2000). *What matters most: The power of living your values.* New York, NY: Fireside.

Practice Happiness 5
Don't let yourself be pigeon-holed

Learn to:
❖ Avoid owning others' expectations of you
❖ Challenge your own expectations of yourself
❖ Avoid comparing yourself to others

---

1. Don't take ownership of others' expectations of you

How often do you hear the following comments, "As work colleagues I expect you to agree with me", "We expect you to follow the career path laid down by your father", "As my husband I expect you to know what I want", or "I expect you to want to spend your free time with me". Expectations are only desired goals and in this case they are someone else's goals, not your own. Personal empowerment is all about focusing on things within your control and being under the thumb of others' expectations of you is certainly not that.

What are some of the expectations your fellow workers or your partner place upon you? Do you think they are fair and reasonable expectations (e.g. equal pay for equal work) or are they unfair? (e.g. the wife who works full-time must also do more of the home duties)

_____

_____

2. Challenge your own expectations

The following expectation thoughts are pretty common: "I should be making as much money as the other managers in the company", "By the age of thirty I expected to have a handsome husband and two adorable children", "At my age I should have the mortgage paid off, own two family cars, and be able to afford an overseas holiday each year" and "I should be as happy as he is, after all we both live in exclusive neighborhoods". But are they healthy expectations?

You should regularly check that you are living YOUR expectations, that they are realistic, and that they are aligned with your values. What are some expectations you place upon yourself?

_____

_____

Regularly challenge your expectations. Is there any evidence why they should be true? Are they aligned with your values?

3. Avoid comparing yourself to others

Realize that the circumstances in your life exist because of the choices you have made. You have made different choices to your friends (based on different values and priorities) and so it stands to reason that you will be on a different path to them. Comparing yourself to others is pointless. Stay focused on your own journey by being sure of your strengths, being passionate about what gives your life meaning, and then trusting in your values. *Other activities in this section discuss strategies for identifying your strengths and values and realizing your life purpose.*

4. Don't take yourself too seriously

Life is a game to be played, not a problem to be fixed. And the game never finishes. The world will continue to turn quite happily without you stressing over deadlines and traffic jams. So make sure you find ways to enjoy every day of the game. Take time out to do enjoyable and fun things for yourself, be it exercise, watching a movie, fishing, visiting friends, or surprising your partner.

What are 5 things you do to help you unwind when you find yourself getting *waaaay* too serious?

_____

_____

5. Give yourself a standing ovation for taking the road less traveled

Be proud of the decisions you are choosing to make to be true to yourself and for following your life purpose. It would be very easy to remain ignorant of your passion and your calling and to stay on the hamster wheel just marking time. But no, you have made the commitment to follow the more difficult route requiring more risk and uncertainty. Be happy. And stand tall!

Practice Happiness 6
Be your very own cheer squad

Learn to:
❖ Be proud of your efforts
❖ Accept that there are no mistakes, just results
❖ Be your own best friend
❖ Treasure and care for your body

---

1. Develop a motivating environment and immerse yourself in it

Choose to feed yourself a regular diet of motivating self-help materials including motivational biographies and documentaries, as well as inspirational media stories-blogs of people who have overcome the odds to reach their goals. Limit your exposure to people and forms of media (particularly the mainstream press) which constantly espouse negativity and stories of doom and gloom. Instead surround yourself with people who are optimistic and who share positive uplifting personal experiences. Also, listen to upbeat music and place motivational posters in your home and at your workplace. Insert links to cheerful and buoyant stories from the Internet on your Facebook site.

What are some things you can begin doing to add more motivational muscle to your lifestyle?

_____

_____

2. Acknowledge all your efforts

So, maybe you tried and you didn't succeed. The point is you had the courage to try. Acknowledge all of your efforts. They will give you the courage to persist. Persistence is just another habit. If you were successful in the past when striving for a goal then you can, and will, be successful again. Believe it. Know it. Now, keep going. Do it!

What is a project you are having difficulty with at the moment?

_____

_____

Now be your own number 1 fan. What are all the things you have going for you in completing the project? (skills, past achievements in similar area, supportive personality traits like persistence, supportive family and friends, loving partner) List all the things that will help you succeed.

_____

_____

3. There are no mistakes, just results

Whenever you don't succeed in accomplishing a goal, look at the outcome or the results. Always ask yourself *"What is the lesson? What can I learn from this experience? How can I benefit from this?"* Then act on those results by changing your behavior accordingly and try again. And then try again. And keep trying until you reach your goal. Choose to view all your attempts as opportunities for growth and for self-discovery, and not as signs of failure or reasons why you should give up on your goal.

4. Be your own best friend

This is instrumental to being your very own cheer squad. Celebrate every success no matter how small and show yourself compassion when you don't succeed. We don't speak to our friends the way we sometimes chastise ourselves. Make it a habit of *talking yourself up*, not talking yourself down. Look at the way Olympic athletes are supported by their cheer squads when they make a mistake – they are immediately encouraged and then told to refocus on the next event.

Create your own best friend mantras. Here are some examples.

- "I can do this….I AM doing this"
- "I succeeded before and I'll succeed again"
- "I'm taking small steps in a forward direction"
- "Every result is a valuable lesson I am learning from"

5. Enlist the support of family and friends

Tell them your goals and let them know the expectations you have of them. You want them to praise *your efforts*, not just your successes.

You want them to regularly enquire about your progress towards your goals. This will help you remain committed to your project.

6. Treasure and care for your body

All your goals and dreams depend upon you being physical healthy. Don't take your health for granted. You know how lousy you feel when you're sick or injured. Do your very best to prevent that from occurring. LOVE your body. Here are some suggestions:

- Carry out cardio workouts 3-4 times per week. These may involve cardiovascular exercise such as running or swimming or cycling or fast walking, or muscle endurance activities, or even a combination of both.

- Every day do some stretching exercises to maintain your flexibility and combat the inactivity of a sedentary lifestyle.

- Ensure you follow a balanced food plan containing sufficient fruit and vegetables and servings of non-battered fish and skinless chicken.

- Never skip meals – this is when we have a tendency to binge on snack and junk food leading to weight gain.

- Drink about 8 to 10 glasses of water each day and limit your alcohol intake to one glass per day.

- Kick the smoking habit and sleep between 6 to 8 hours per day.

Caring for your body will not only provide you with numerous well-established physiological benefits, but will also help you sleep better, improve your concentration, be more resilient when tackling problems, boost your self-confidence, and give you unlimited reserves of energy. In a nutshell, it will greatly improve your quality of life.

Set up a sleep schedule for yourself. (For example, I finish eating 3 hours before hopping into bed each night at 10 and then read for 30 minutes. I sleep wonderfully and wake up fully refreshed the next morning, *hungry for action*.)

Others will notice the way you treat yourself. If you want others to treat you with respect first you need to show yourself respect. Here are 6 tips.

- Dress appropriately for the occasion
- Walk tall and with confidence
- Solicit and listen to the opinion of others with respect and without judgment
- Speak to be heard – with confidence and upright body posture
- Assertively communicate your needs and your expectations of others
- Care for your body with regular exercise and a healthy food plan

---

Practice Happiness 7
Find a cause greater than yourself

Learn to:

❖ Discover a charitable cause that interests you
❖ See all the benefits you will gain from committing
 to your cause
❖ Commit to your cause

All of the exercises for this story are concerned with finding a charitable cause to which you may donate some of your skills and time. Practice Happiness 8 focuses on helping a person find a job that can lead to a more meaningful life and sense of purpose.

1. Find a greater cause than yourself

(a) First, study your values and your strengths and decide which field you wish to invest your energy in. Some examples include corporate volunteering, volunteering for a charity, volunteering for an environmental group, event volunteering, or international volunteering. Any initial thoughts?

(b) Second, conduct a Google search in your area of interest. This will give you a list of charities, groups, and companies as well as past projects people have worked on.

(c) Third, consider your time availability. Are you interested in one-off events (e.g. Oxfam Trailwalker conducted over 2 days in teams,

Smith Family Xmas Gift Deliveries done in a morning, Red Cross Calling Appeal involving door knocking for half a day, making a blood donation every 3 months)? Or a regular weekly volunteering effort (e.g. providing support at a mental illness accommodation center, helping out in the tuck shop at a primary school, being an official at Little Athletics carnivals, writing campaign articles for a community organization)? Or perhaps a commitment over a much longer time frame (e.g. raising puppies for Guide Dogs Victoria, tutoring asylum refugees in English, being a classroom helper in schools, planting trees for local councils)?

If your job or lifestyle makes it difficult to commit to a weekly cause try a one-off event every few months. Even better, stroll down the road right now and talk to one of your local charity groups about how you might be able to help them.

The following tips will help you remain committed to your cause.

- If your cause is a one-off event lasting one or two days start by contacting your friends and try and organize a team. You will be able to motivate each other.
- Tell others about your goal and its importance.

Tips continued.

- Appreciate how your contribution will benefit others – this will help keep you committed and bolster your own self-esteem.
- During the actual event reward yourself for each little forward step and every day visualize yourself reaching your goal.
- Consider recruiting some friends to your cause. Start a team.
- Remember the other valuable benefits of committing to your cause: learning new skills, meeting new friends, boosting your career options, and enjoying a sense of achievement.

Extra Resources

Blaustein, A. I. (2003). *Make a difference: America's guide to volunteering and community service.* San Francisco, CA: Jossey-Bass.

Friedman, J. (2003). *The busy family's guide to volunteering: Do good, have fun, make a difference as a family!* Beltsville, MD: Robins Lane Press.

Lonely Planet. (2013). *Volunteer: A traveler's guide to making a difference around the world.* Melbourne, Australia: Lonely Planet.

Practice Happiness 8
Live a life of meaning and enjoy a meaningful life

Learn to:
❖ Define your own life purpose
❖ Identify a job you are passionate about
❖ Align your purpose with your values to enjoy greater happiness and motivation

1. Write your own eulogy

If you died today what would your eulogy consist of? What 5 qualities would your friends use to describe you? (put yourself in *their* shoes)

_____

_____

What 5 qualities would you prefer your friends use to describe you?

_____

_____

What would be your 5 major lifetime achievements? And are they what you wish to be remembered for?

_____

_____

What things would you have to start doing differently for your life to start reflecting your preferred qualities and achievements?

_____

_____

2. Define your life purpose or sense of purpose

(a) This involves 5 steps. First, go back and look at your strengths and passions that you recorded earlier in the Practice Happiness 3 exercises. Summarize your strengths below.

_____

_____

What causes do you strongly believe in? (Some examples include the underprivileged, animal welfare, environment causes, and community groups. Your values may help you answering this question.)

_____

_____

If you could deliver a message to a large group of people who would those people be and what would be your message?

_____

_____

(b) What do you want to do? (Look back at your strengths and passions and then frame your answer in a sentence using an action verb. Some examples of action verbs include translate, communicate, create, present, compute, analyze, train, teach, supervise, administer, collect, diagnose, program.)

_____

_____

(c) Who do you want to help? Look back at your values and causes for ideas.

_____

_____

(d) What will be the outcome of the action you perform with your designated group? What value will you create? What will be the result of your efforts?

_____

_____

(e) Combine your answers from the previous three questions into one or two sentences. This will represent your current life purpose. An example might be: "My life purpose is to educate and motivate unemployed youth to gain meaningful and fulfilling employment."

_____

_____

3. Find a job you are passionate about and which is meaningful to you

Instead of allowing yourself to be pigeon-holed in a job that doesn't quite meet your qualifications or satisfy your passions you can try these two methods to land that dream job.

- One, identify both your strengths and a cause you believe in (e.g. improving education opportunities for the underprivileged, teaching obese people healthier lifestyle habits, designing more environmentally-friendly resorts), and then find a company that satisfies both of these.

- Two, find a company that services a cause you believe in and approach them directly. Then inform them about the unique nature of your strengths and detail the ways that you will add value to their company.

Having established your life purpose, updated your resume, and found those companies that are dedicated to your own cause approach them directly. Dress to impress and just GO. Sell yourself big time.

4. Remember that your sense of purpose must align with your values

For your life purpose to remain meaningful and to continue to motivate you it is important that *your purpose aligns with your higher values*. Consequently, every decision you make will reflect your values which will result in greater feelings of happiness and fulfillment. If your value hierarchy changes, because of the arrival of a family's first child or perhaps a new mortgage, then your life purpose may also change and may have to be redefined.

Extra Resources

Bolles, R. N. (2013). *What color is your parachute? 2014: A practical manual for job-hunters and career-changers*. Berkeley, California: Ten Speed Press.

Step

2

Live with a Positive Attitude

See the world with a sunny
confident outlook

In this step

Adopt empowering beliefs that increase your confidence

*

Develop springboard thoughts that propel you towards your goals

*

Manage your own stress

*

Learn to avoid taking on the stress of others

*

Are your expectations controlling your happiness?

*

Be happy with your progress, not just your outcomes

*

Look for a benefit in every situation

*

Understand that the world is your mirror

*

Learn to be comfortable with change and uncertainty

*

Feelings of discomfort signal approaching opportunities

Practice Happiness 9
Your beliefs influence your feelings

Learn to:
❖ Identify the limiting beliefs holding you back
❖ Challenge your limiting beliefs
❖ Replace your limiting beliefs with empowering
  beliefs that increase your confidence

---

1. Identify the beliefs behind your own feelings

Your feelings act as a barometer allowing you to gauge your internal weather of thoughts and beliefs. Your beliefs direct your thoughts which, in turn, direct your feelings. *Change your beliefs and you can take greater control of your feelings!*

Look at Table 4. If you are feeling miserable and are thinking "I don't like my job anymore," you can uncover the belief by simply asking the question "Why don't you like your job anymore?" The reason – the belief – might be "because I am not using my strengths and I don't find the work meaningful." Using the same process you can now identify all of your beliefs behind your feelings, paying particular attention to the situations where you experience unpleasant emotions. Repeat this process to identify the beliefs behind your own feelings.

Feelings	Thought	Belief
Miserable	I don't like my job anymore	I am not using my strengths and I don't find the work meaningful
Bored	There's nothing to do at the campsite	There are no video games, no TV, none of my school friends, no mobile phones
Excited	I am really looking forward to seeing Barry at the party tonight	Barry and I seem to have so much in common and we chat together so easily

Table 4

2. Are your beliefs helping you or holding you back?

To clarify the usefulness of our beliefs we can divide them into 2 categories: limiting or empowering. In Table 5 you can see several common limiting beliefs that many people choose to live their life by, together with empowering alternatives. Do any of them look familiar?

Limiting belief	Empowering belief
If I make a mistake it's clear proof that I should give up on the project I am working on	Every time I make a mistake I am learning something valuable and am strengthening my resolve
Because of my tumultuous childhood I will never be happy	My parents weren't perfect but my rough childhood has no influence over who I choose to be today
I can never be happy because life is always so unfair	My happiness is not contingent upon luck or hoping things will happen
Unless I am in an intimate relationship I will never be happy	I am happy now focusing on loving myself and being true to myself
To be content in life I must be super successful and rich	I am content knowing that I am pursuing my life purpose and living my values
Holding on to grudges lets people know that I'm no pushover	Instead of holding grudges I will practice compassion and forgiveness
I just don't have enough time to do the things I want to do	After re-examining my priorities I will have enough time to do the things I want to do

Table 5

Limiting beliefs:

- Make other people and events responsible for your present feelings
- Deprive you of having control of your behaviors and feelings leading to loss of self-confidence
- Lead to unpleasant feelings such as frustration and anger
- Keep you stuck in the past (e.g. grudges, previous setbacks)
- Often use language framed in absolutes which lock you into a perception that the situation is hopeless (e.g. never, impossible)
- Use language that act as handbrakes preventing you from exploring other ways of moving forward (e.g. I can't, I mustn't, I

shouldn't)

Empowering beliefs:
- Give you total responsibility for your present feelings
- Give you total control of your thoughts, behaviors and feelings leading to improvements in self-confidence
- Lead to pleasant emotions such as happiness and contentment
- Free you from the mistakes and hurts of your past allowing you to move forward with renewed hope and compassion
- Unleash your creativity to solve problems
- Use language that act as springboards motivating you to explore new ways of moving forward (e.g. I can, I will, it's up to me)

3. Challenge your limiting beliefs
Now that you are able to distinguish limiting beliefs from empowering beliefs it's time for you to challenge those beliefs that are holding you back. Whenever you identify a limiting belief ask yourself the following questions:
- What evidence exists that the belief is true?
- What evidence exists that the belief is not true?
- If I reject the belief, what is the worst thing that can happen to me?
- If I reject the belief, how might my life be better?

What are 3 limiting beliefs that are currently holding you back in your relationship, your family life or at work? Write them down and challenge them.

_____

_____

4. Replace your limiting beliefs with empowering beliefs
Here is where you get to lay down a framework of beliefs that will guarantee you greater happiness. Using the limiting beliefs you

identified earlier transform them into empowering beliefs that excite you and fill you with optimism.

_____

_____

5. Test drive your new empowering beliefs

For each of your new beliefs ask yourself the following questions: "If I believed the new belief, what new thoughts would I have? How would I behave differently? How would I feel?" Complete this process for several of your new empowering beliefs. An example has been done for you in Table 6.

Feelings	New behaviors	New thoughts	Empowering belief
Happy; optimistic; hopeful	I would take more risks; I would be more adventurous; I take things less personally	How can I benefit from this setback? I'm looking forward to this opportunity I haven't tried this before – GREAT!	There are no mistakes or failures, only results

Table 6

Turn your new beliefs into habits. Type them on to your computer desktop, place them on your Smartphone and iPad, write them down on sticky notes and place them around your home and in your car. Read them and say them out loud every chance you get. And then congratulate yourself when you taste the benefits of a new belief. You are the reason for the improvements in your life. YOU.

Extra Resources

Ellis, A. (2001). *Feeling better, getting better, staying better: Profound self-help therapy for your emotions.* Atascadero, CA: Impact Publishers.

Ellis, A. (2001). *Overcoming destructive beliefs, feelings, and behaviors.* Amherst, NY: Prometheus Books.

Practice Happiness 10

Free your mind of handbrake thoughts that hold you back

Learn to:

❖ Identify your handbrake thoughts
❖ Identify the associated limiting beliefs
❖ Challenge your limiting beliefs
❖ Replace your handbrake thoughts with springboard thoughts that empower you

---

1. Identify your use of handbrake thoughts

Pay close attention to your thoughts. Do you use words such as "I can't", "I don't", "I won't", "I shouldn't", "I mustn't", "I ought to" or absolutes like "never" and "impossible"? As soon as you say you can't do something your brain does two things – first, it begins searching for evidence to support why you can't do something, and second, you become blind to the possibility of success. See the examples in Table 7.

Now try and identify some of your own handbrake words with the probable associated limiting beliefs.

Handbrake thought	Associated limiting belief
I can't complete the project by the deadline	I was late completing the last 2 projects (and my colleagues always miss deadlines too)
I don't do outdoor adventure activities	I was never allowed to do outdoor adventure activities as a child
I never have any luck meeting men at parties	Men think I am boring (and I don't think nice single men attend parties anyway)

Table 7

2. Challenge the beliefs associated with your handbrake thoughts

If you do use any of the handbrake words immediately challenge them by asking yourself the following questions.

- What evidence exists for the associated limiting belief?
- How can you be so certain that you won't succeed at the task?
- Why can't you complete the task?
- What evidence is there that you can't achieve a goal?
- And if you can't achieve the goal right now, why can't you achieve the goal in the future (with more training, more funds, more contacts)?
- Now, what evidence is there for a new empowering belief? (past successes, your qualifications, discipline, creativity, supportive family and friends)

Do you have any handbrake thoughts that are currently holding you back in a particular area of your life? Write down the associated limiting beliefs and then challenge these beliefs.

_____

_____

Just because you couldn't do something in the past does not mean you cannot succeed the next time. Remember also that successes are always built upon numerous trials. Rarely does anyone succeed with their first attempt.

3. Avoid using grey language

Be wary of using words such as "probably", "I'll try", "maybe", and "I wish". Such words lack commitment and suggest that you are relying on luck and the lottery to achieve your goal. You are the captain of your ship. Take control. As Yoda said, "There is no try, just do or do not."

4. Replace your handbrake thoughts with springboard thoughts

This activity will teach you to replace thoughts associated with unhappy emotions (handbrake thoughts) with thoughts associated with happy emotions (springboard thoughts). Develop the habit of using positive present and future-oriented language such as "I can", "I will", and "I shall". Ideally, use the term "I am" as often as possible as it expresses commitment and anchors you in the present.

Consider the earlier example about a looming project deadline. Worrying and getting stressed is pointless, wasting both your energy and time. Remember that you always have control over your thoughts and, thus, your emotions. So, focus on the things that would allow you to complete the project on time. These springboard thoughts will immediately give you feelings of optimism.

Recall some of the occasions when you find yourself using handbrake thoughts. Then change them to springboard thoughts. The example in Table 8 will help you.

Situation	Feelings	Handbrake thought	Springboard thought
Approaching deadline for a project	Tense, anxious	I can't complete the project by the deadline.	I will complete the project in time. I will see Tim who has been involved in similar projects before. Also I will delegate some of my other work to my colleagues.

Table 8

5. Tell others about your goal-related springboard thoughts

One of your greatest resources when striving for goals and remaining future-focused is the support and encouragement of your family and friends. Involve them in your efforts and request their assistance. Telling them about your goal is also a wonderful way for you to publicly commit yourself to your goals and your deadlines.

Tell your partner or one of your closest friends of a personal goal that is very important to you. Tell this person also of your springboard thoughts that are going to support your efforts. Convince them why you will succeed.

6. Recruit supporters

Surround yourself with people who believe in your endeavors. They will support you through the tough times when your commitment wavers and help keep you focused. Stay clear of doubters, particularly those who have never achieved your goal. Also, talk to people who have accomplished a similar goal to yours and ask their advice.

Extra Resources

Ellis, A. (2001). *Feeling better, getting better, staying better: Profound self-help therapy for your emotions.* Atascadero, CA: Impact Publishers.

Ellis, A. (2001). *Overcoming destructive beliefs, feelings, and behaviors.* Amherst, NY: Prometheus Books.

Practice Happiness 11
Inoculate yourself against secondhand stress

Learn to:
❖ Identify the origin of your own stress
❖ Manage your own stress
❖ See if you are a magnet for stressed people
❖ Avoid taking on the stress of others

---

1. Identifying the origin of your stress

The first step in learning to deal with secondhand stress is to clearly identify the origin of your stress. Is your stress from another person responding to their own problems (an anxious boss, frustrated car drivers, your moaning friend) or is your stress a response to your own problems (your own deadlines and dilemmas)? Once you know this then you can decide what action to take. If your stress is from someone else remember that you have no control over their emotions. Neither are you responsible for their emotions. At any time you can choose not to take on board their stress. On the other hand, if the stress is your own, you can manage it by changing your own thoughts and behaviors.

Table 9 shows how you can pinpoint the origin of your stress for any situations by identifying the associated automatic thoughts.

Feelings	Physical symptoms	Situation	Automatic thought	Origin of stress
Frustration	Jittery	Mike talks to me at my desk at work.	Oh no, Mike's complaining about his girlfriend again.	Mike
Disappointment	Hollow emptiness, deflated	The boss criticized my report.	I'm hopeless.	Me
Tense	Fast shallow breathing	Stuck in traffic jam in John's car on the way to work.	I wish John would stop moaning about the traffic jam.	John

Table 9

You are not responsible for another person's emotions, thoughts, or beliefs.

2. Managing your own stress

You may find that particular situations, not people, are causing you stress. Are you overly sensitive to sad or romantic films? Do you feel on edge in big crowds? Are you depressed after watching the evening news? Do you lose it when you have to wait in queues? If so, you may have to learn to distance yourself from certain situations. At the same time take charge of your own reactions to stressful situations by managing your beliefs, thoughts, and feelings. Your Feelings Diary from Practice Happiness 1 will help you.

If you choose the compassion route and decide to listen to someone who needs to vent their troubles consider the following tips to safeguard your own emotional wellbeing.

- Just listen. Only offer advice if requested. Getting involved in the solution is a guaranteed way of catching the other person's stress.

- You may find it necessary to set boundaries with the person. This means letting them know what help, if any, you are prepared to offer. Let them know that you can be a sounding board and offer advice but that if it turns into a nonstop litany of whining and moaning you will not be able to help them any further.

- To help prevent incessant grumbling, try injecting positivity into the conversation. If the person asks for advice encourage them to look for a silver lining, get them to acknowledge their strengths, and help them devise a plan of action.

- You can assist them in managing their own stress by giving them a copy of this book.

- You can model how to maintain calm behavior in a crisis in front of them.

3. Are you a magnet for stressed individuals?

You may find that the same people keep using you as an emotional garbage dump. They may be attracted to your perceived strength, your compassionate nature, or your lack of assertiveness. While the attention can seem flattering at first, it can quickly drain your emotional energy. There is the additional danger that the same persons will continue dumping on you again and again. If this happens consider the following suggestions.

- Start by re-examining your values. Do you only feel valued when listening to the worries of others? Does it make you feel needed? If so, perhaps you need to start valuing yourself in more respecting and self-affirming ways.
- If you choose to continue helping lots of people in need try being more selective about whom you help and how you help them.

> The next time you help someone who is stressed examine your feelings. Do you feel energized and invigorated or do you feel drained and used? If you find that a particular person makes you feel drained and empty let them know: "When I listen to you I find that I'm picking up some of your own stress." The other person may not even be aware of their effect on you and may appreciate your observation. This may help preserve the friendship too.

4. Don't pass on secondhand stress to others

When we're infected with a virus we don't go out of our way to make others sick do we? Of course not, so here is your chance to stop the virus dead in its tracks. Resist the urge to pass on the gossip or negativity that infected you. Focus instead on maintaining a regular diet of positivity in your life. Pass on good news, happy uplifting stories of hope and achievement. *Be the person that others look forward to seeing at the coffee bar because you energize people and make them feel good about life.*

5. Care for yourself

When you skip meals, burn the candle at both ends, and neglect social interaction your immunity system is weakened and you are most vulnerable to colds and nasty infections. Taking care of yourself is your most important defense against secondhand stress. Continue to practice relaxing breathing, get sufficient sleep, exercise regularly, follow a healthy food plan, spend time with your positive friends, and love yourself.

Extra Resources

Benson, H. (2000). *The relaxation response.* New York, NY: HarperTorch.

Ford, J., & Wortmann, J. (2013). *Hijacked by your brain: How to free yourself when stress takes over.* Naperville, ILL: Sourcebooks.

Spradlin, S. E. (2003). *Don't let your emotions run your life: How dialectical behavior therapy can put you in control.* Oakland, CA: New Harbinger Publications.

Practice Happiness 12

Don't let your expectations control your happiness

Learn to:

❖ Realize the futility of thinking "I'll be happy when…."

❖ Realize that fairness is entirely your own interpretation

❖ Focus on your progress instead of solely on your outcomes

❖ Keep a Gratitude Diary

---

1. Don't make your happiness dependent upon meeting the expectations of others

Sometimes we place our own happiness in the hands of others. We tell ourselves the following things:

"*I'll be happy when* other people accept me for who I am"

"*I'll be happy when* other people please me"

"*I'll be happy when* other people return my kindness or my favors"

"*I'll be happy when* other people are like me"

"*I'll be happy when* other people treat me the way I deserve to be treated"

But remember that you can't control the thoughts, behaviors, and emotions of others so *expecting others* to think, behave or feel a certain way can only lead to one outcome – disappointment and frustration for you. Never let your happiness be dependent upon the actions or the expectations of others.

2. Ditch the sentence "I'll be happy when......." from your vocabulary

Setting realistic expectations for ourselves about things we have control over (our best performance; honesty; integrity; reliability; trust) can be motivating and encourage us to raise our personal standards. The problem is when we tell ourselves that we will only be happy when we *meet* our expectations.

How often have you heard people say the following statements?

"*I'll be happy when* I meet the man of my dreams"

"*I'll be happy when* I get married"

"*I'll be happy when* I can afford to buy a house"

"*I'll be happy when* I get that promotion"

"*I'll be happy when* I have a family with two kids"

"I'll be happy when the weekend comes around"

"*I'll be happy when* the kids are old enough to go to school"

"*I'll be happy when* I finish writing that book"

"*I'll be happy when* I can retire"

Telling yourself that you will only be happy when you meet certain expectations is postponing your happiness for a future time that may never arrive. Know that you can be, and deserve to be, happy at any time. (And make the most of your health while you have it too.) Being happy today will also greatly increase your chances of reaching your expectations anyway as you will be helping to maintain your motivation.

3. Realize that thinking in terms of fairness is a pointless endeavor

Recently I copped a parking fine. I misread a parking sign, parked the car outside a shop, went into the shop, came out 5 minutes later only to find a $144 ticket waiting for me on my windshield. Was it unfair? No way. It was my fault. Plain and simple. Fairness had nothing to do with it. At other times we are just in the wrong place at the wrong time. Like when another motorist slammed into the back of my car. It was entirely his fault but it left me without the use of my car for the next three weeks. Was it unfair? Of course not. It was neither fair nor unfair. It just happened. What was important is how I chose to *interpret* the situation afterwards. Instead of wasting time and energy dwelling about why it happened to me I decided to focus on finding a benefit. Hey, it happened, right? I might as well get something useful from the experience. I'll tell you about the benefits in the next story.

> Don't waste time and energy lost in pointless fairness thinking. Focus on finding a benefit.

4. Be happy with your growth instead of focusing on outcomes

Okay, so you want to get that promotion that's up for grabs at the office. But rather than focus on the end-point – getting the promotion – be happy with your efforts and your professional development as you go for the promotion. Find happiness now.

Look at the examples in Table 10 and then repeat the exercise with some of your own current expectations or goals.

Expectation or goal	Delayed happiness	Happiness now
Paying off the mortgage.	I'll be happy when I have paid off the mortgage.	*I'm happy now because* each week I'm gradually paying off the mortgage.
Meeting the right woman for a healthy loving relationship.	I'll be happy when I meet the right woman for a healthy loving relationship.	*I'm happy now because* I'm making efforts to meet the right woman by joining clubs, expanding my network of friends, and accepting all the social invitations I receive.
Getting a promotion.	I'll be happy when I get a promotion.	*I'm happy now* because I'm improving my value as an employee by taking night classes, shadowing a mentor at work, and volunteering for extra leadership duties.

Table 10

5. Be grateful for what you have now

Don't make your happiness dependent upon something that may or may not happen in the future. Stop being so future-oriented in your thinking and learn to be grounded in the present – because that is where happiness is! You have many reasons to be happy right now.

Consider keeping a Gratitude Diary. Every day jot down 5 things you are grateful for. What are 5 things you are grateful for today? (e.g. your family, having your health, having a job, living in a democratic country, having friendly neighbors, being able to drop in on your mother for coffee)

_____

_____

> ## Practice Happiness 13
> *Look for a silver lining in every cloud*
>
> ### Learn to:
> ❖ See that how you choose to interpret a situation determines your emotions
> ❖ See that all situations, regardless of their scale or circumstances, are neither good nor bad
> ❖ Look for the benefit in any situation

1. How you interpret the situation is up to you

Realize that you are responsible for the value and meaning you attach to events in your life. *They are neither good nor bad in themselves.* If a millionaire and a university student each crash their car each will probably have a very different outlook. The millionaire might just shrug his shoulders as he can easily buy another car, while the student has all his money wrapped up in his car and panics. Alternatively, the millionaire's car may be his pride and joy, while the student planned on selling his car for a bicycle. The point is it is your choice how upset, relieved, or nonchalant you want to feel afterwards. If you want to react like it's the end of the world that's fine. If you want to just shrug your shoulders that's fine. Or if you want to see it as one of life's valuable lessons then that's fine as well. *Your choice.*

The next time you suffer a 'misfortune' (whether it's a car accident, a washed out picnic, losing your phone, or missing the train) refuse to take the victim stance ("Why me?") or play the fairness card ("This is so unfair!"). Remind yourself that nothing is good or bad in itself. Look for the lesson.

2. How can you benefit from the situation?

Instead of thinking to yourself about all the ways you will be disadvantaged, ask yourself how the situation could work to your advantage. Another motorist recently crashed into the back of my car. Even though the accident was the other driver's fault I was the one penalized being without my car for three weeks as it sat at the panel beater's workshop. However, I was determined to find a benefit. I asked myself the question, "What will this force me to do that I might not otherwise do?" Over the next three weeks I rediscovered the public transport system, made some new friends, rode my bicycle a lot more improving my fitness, and my car received a lovely new paint job. It's all about perspective.

Following the examples set out in Table 11 describe 5 setbacks you have recently experienced in your life. What is a potential benefit you found in each?

_____

_____

Setback	Usual outcome	Potential benefit
A friend lied about you to others.	Hold a grudge and refuse to talk to them for the next month.	You can learn compassion, to forgive the person who wronged you.
You hurt your back playing with your kids	Focus on the inconvenience of having an injury and make a mental note not to play with the kids anymore.	Remember to warm up, do regular exercise and flexibility exercises, and adopt better postural habits.
You lose your Smartphone.	Get super angry and think it's the end of the world.	Rethink your obsession with material possessions, reflect on your values.

Table 11

Practice Happiness 14
Wherever you go, there you are

Learn to:
❖ Understand that your habitual thought patterns and behaviors follow you wherever you go
❖ Realize that you play a key role in any recurring patterns in your life
❖ See that the way you think and behave is reflected back at you by the world around you

---

1. Accept that you will never be able to escape from yourself

This is the crux of the statement "Wherever you go, there you are." No matter where you go or how different the geography or the people, *your habitual thought patterns and behaviors go with you*. Once you realize this, and fully accept its implications, then you can focus on modifying what you can change about yourself - your thought patterns, your behaviors, and your values.

2. Be happy with where you are right now

Do you sometimes find yourself wondering if the grass is greener on the other side of the fence? Do you have those moments when you wonder if you would be happier and more content if you were somewhere else, or with someone else, or doing something else, or being someone else? In truth, the something else that you need is being able to live more fully in the present. You can achieve this by learning to better appreciate your present situation – your job, your partner, your house, your neighborhood, your friends, your strengths. Regularly keeping a Gratitude Diary is one idea. *You will find many other useful strategies for developing a present-oriented state of mind in Step 3.*

3. Look out for recurring patterns in your life

Your thoughts that follow you everywhere are either supporting your endeavors or they are sabotaging you. So when you notice recurring patterns in your life….PAY ATTENTION.

- Do you find that your initial excitement at starting a new job or project is replaced by boredom shortly after?
- Do all of your relationships break up after 6 months?
- Do you always feel lethargic and down in the dumps within a month of returning from vacations?
- Do you find that your initial excitement at buying something (a car, a home theatre system, a dress, a pair of shoes) is always replaced by a feeling of emptiness shortly after?
- Do you find that every time you move cities that initial sense of adventure is soon replaced by the old feelings of routine and boredom?

If any of these apply to you, your attitudes are the most likely culprit. Take the time to examine your beliefs and thoughts related to the recurring pattern that you wish to change. Look for limiting beliefs and handbrake thoughts that are sabotaging you. You may have to replace these with empowering beliefs and springboard thoughts that support your goals. *See the exercises at the start of Step 2.*

Also, examine your values. Are you living every day the values you associate with the type of relationship you want? Is your new car reflected in your top values? *You may wish to re-examine the activities in Step 1 that deal with value hierarchy development.*

4. Recapture your upbeat attitudes from your vacation

People will tell you that they are often happiest and they like themselves more when on holiday. They are more non-judgmental, more compassionate, they take more risks, they are more resilient when faced with setbacks, they go with the flow, they go out of their way to interact with strangers, and they take advantage of opportunities that arise. You can access these positive and empowering attitudes at any point in time to enjoy a happier state of mind. Why only be this happy on holidays?

Think back to one of your happiest vacations. What beliefs and thought patterns were you probably thinking each day?

_____

_____

5. The world is your mirror

One very good way to gauge how healthfully you perceive the world is to monitor the reactions of people whom you come into contact. For example, if you smile at someone, chances are they will return your smile. If you behave aggressively with someone be aware that they will probably act aggressively towards you. If you spend all your time whining to friends about your lot in life don't be surprised when you get an earful of the same sort of negativity from them. If you notice that so few people seem to display generosity towards you, it's probably because you show very little generosity to others.

Think of a time in your weekly routine when you are in the company of others and all of you are happy. What thoughts and behaviors are you displaying that are probably contributing to the happy atmosphere?

_____

_____

Now think of a time in your weekly routine when you are in the company of others and all of you are less than happy. What thoughts and behaviors are you displaying in this case?

_____

_____

The way you think and behave is reflected back at you by the world outside. So if you want to change the emotional atmosphere first change yourself.

For one whole day smile at every person you come into contact with. Not only that, give a hearty greeting to all these people too. Try it. You'll be amazed at the results (and at the doors it will open).

Extra Resources

Young, J. E., & Klosko, J. S. (1994). *Reinventing your life: The breakthrough program to end negative behavior and feel great again*. New York, NY: Plume.

Practice Happiness 15
Be comfortable with not knowing the future

Learn to:
❖ Make change your friend
❖ Ask three questions when facing uncertainty
❖ See that feelings of discomfort often signal approaching opportunities
❖ Realize that you always have options

---

1. Become comfortable with the present moment

Accept where you are right NOW. Don't think of what you might be doing in a minute's time. Don't get caught up in agonizing over all the possible future scenarios and outcomes. Learn to live in the present by totally immersing yourself in individual tasks and being aware of all your senses. Pretty soon you will discover that the uncertain future is far out of your mind and seems far less threatening.

2. Make it a habit to step outside your comfort zone

What worries most of us about an uncertain future is the prospect of change. We are very resistant when it comes to changing our lives and our routines. The way to tackle this is to *make change your friend.* Constantly keep pushing your boundaries by trying new foods, increasing the intensity or duration of your exercise bouts, talking to people in unfamiliar environments, writing for longer periods of time, committing to more challenging personal development courses. Experimenting in one area will also give you the confidence to experiment in other areas. And always reward yourself for all your efforts.

What are 5 simple things you could do differently this week to become more comfortable with the idea of change?

You feel most alive when you step outside of your comfort zone because that is when you are growing and learning new things about yourself!

3. When facing uncertainty keep in mind these 3 questions

One, can you control or influence the situation? If not, waste no further time or energy on it. Stay focused on the things you can control or change.

Two, is the situation important enough to warrant further effort on your part? If it isn't, let it go.

Three, is it related to my values and vision? If it isn't important or is unrelated to your mission in the bigger scheme of things, let it go.

Staying true to your values is the compass that will keep you on track and feeling comfortable during those moments when you aren't sure which path to take. Have faith in your values. Ensure your behaviors and thoughts reflect your values. And then listen to your instincts because they will alert you if you are in danger of straying from your course. *You may wish to have another look at the Step 1 activities.*

4. Feelings of discomfort may be alerting you to opportunities

Expect to feel sore, uneasy, or anxious when entering uncharted territory. You are having these feelings because you are being invited to step outside of your comfort zone. So, at these times, rather than distracting yourself or avoiding the situation, develop the habit of asking yourself, "What is the opportunity for me here?"

5. Always face uncertainty from a position of strength

Whenever tackling a task laced with uncertainty do a quick stock take of your strengths that will support you going forward – identify your support network, restate your vision and values, remind yourself of your past successes that were also preceded by initial periods of uncertainty (sporting achievements, enjoyable dates, successful job interviews, rush projects that were completed). These will be your anchors in the tough times ahead.

6. Know that you're not seeing every option

When we are confronted with uncertain situations our natural reaction is to start trying to read the future. The more important the situation to us the more anxious we become as we begin considering all the possible negative scenarios. Instead, as soon as uncertainty strikes, relax using techniques such as abdominal breathing, meditation, yoga, or exercise. Then, after establishing a position of strength, as discussed previously, calmly remind yourself that there are countless options available to you, many of which you may be blind to at the present moment. Be patient.

7. Be comfortable with making mistakes

Remember that there are no mistakes, only results. And results provide necessary feedback you need to reach your goal. The faster you get the results the sooner you will achieve your goal. So embrace mistakes, or results, as useful learning opportunities. Nothing of real importance or value was ever gained without mistakes. If you're not making any mistakes, you're doing something wrong.

8. You don't need to have the whole picture to act

In a world based on technological change and shifting alliances realize that you will never have all the information you need for complete certainty. Don't miss a valuable opportunity by waiting to have all the pieces. Get as much information as you can within the time available to you, make the best decision you can, and then act. At least then you're in play. You can always modify your plan as you go along.

What is an area in your life you have been postponing until you had all the pieces? (e.g. a new business venture, asking a man out on a date, starting home renovations, a new exercise program)

_____

_____

Write down all the reasons why you should start the project NOW
and all the things that will support you.

_____

_____

9. Get excited about the opportunities that accompany uncertainty

Keep reminding yourself that moments of uncertainty herald periods
of self-growth as well as opportunities to learn about yourself, realize
new strengths, discover new hobbies, make new friends, and develop
new networks of contacts in the business world.

Think of an opportunity that has come your
way recently (at work, at home, concerning
friends) that you have yet to make a decision.
Weigh up the *possible benefits* of doing
something against the probable costs of doing
nothing. Visualize where this opportunity
could take you if you are bold enough to grab
it and possess the energy to run with it. The
possibilities….

Extra Resources

Ballach, S., & Brede, A. (2011). *Get out of your comfort zone: The exercise book for your personal growth*. CreateSpace: Amazon.

Jeffers, S. (2006). *Feel the fear and do it anyway*. New York, NY: Ballantine Books.

Practice Happiness 16

Beware of stereotypes

Learn to:

❖ Challenge stereotypes

❖ Look for the wonders hidden by stereotypes

❖ Distance yourself from those spreading harmful stereotypes

---

1. Identify the fear or insecurity supporting the stereotype

People perpetuate stereotypes for a reason. Behind every stereotype is a fear of the unknown. Fear of perhaps a cultural group or a religious group that seem strange to us. Labeling the group with a stereotype allows us to justify our own behaviors as being "more correct." But all we are doing is shortchanging ourselves of a more enriched life. Stereotypes rob us of compassion for others and lock us into a rigid set of beliefs and judgments which limit our opportunities in life for meeting different types of people and enjoying different types of experiences.

Here is your opportunity to challenge yourself. Think of a stereotype in your own life (e.g. about a person, a religion, an event, a program) and list the reasons why you think people support the stereotype.

_____

_____

2. Challenge the stereotype

Look for evidence opposing the stereotype. This might involve an indirect method of searching the internet, watching documentaries, and doing short courses. Or you may decide upon a more direct method that confronts the stereotype head-on. You might actually try scuba diving with sharks. Or visiting several tattoo parlors. Or talking to Muslims about their beliefs.

Think of a stereotype in your own life. What evidence can you find to oppose the stereotype?

_____

_____

3. Be curious and look for the wonder behind the stereotype

Conduct some research for fascinating facts about the topic. Once you do this you will begin to see the topic in a less threatening way. Your unfounded beliefs will be replaced by a more open and welcoming attitude of marvel and appreciation. Behind every stereotype is untapped happiness....your happiness.

4. Disconnect yourself from those perpetuating the stereotype

To prevent stereotypes from rubbing off on you consider maintaining some distance from those perpetuating them. In particular, take with a grain of salt anything you hear on television or read in newspapers. Remember that the media only broadcasts the exceptions, and the exceptions are inevitably bad news of a sensational nature.

Watch the evening news. Take note of the nature of the stories – the same types of people seem to commit all the indiscretions, certain countries are always responsible for public safety issues, particular cultures produce all the terrorists, all politicians seem to be liars. Also note the language used by the reporters – sensationalist stories full of hyperbole and exaggeration are a dead giveaway of stereotypes.

Step

3

Live in the Present

Savor the moment,
the birthplace of happiness

In this step

Recognize everything you have to be grateful for

*

How to remain young at heart

*

Challenge expectations associated with your age

*

How to still your mind in a busy world

*

How to become a more effective listener

*

How to calm yourself for a good night's sleep

*

How to breathe properly for optimal health and relaxation

*

To be happier you have to laugh more, it's that simple

*

Grudges and resentments rob you of happiness

*

Having *more stuff* will never make you *more happy*

Practice Happiness 17
Start and finish each day with gratitude

Learn to:

❖ Be thankful for all you have in your life

❖ Express your gratitude to others

❖ Role-model acts of gratitude in front of children

---

1. Reflect on what might *not* have been

What if you had never gone to that party and therefore never met your partner? What if you had not received that tip about that job vacancy which ultimately led to you getting your present job? What if you had left the house five minutes earlier and been involved in that car accident on the freeway?

Sit down with a close friend or your partner and discuss how different each of your lives might be if you *had not met each other*. Would you have your current jobs? Would you be living where you are living now? *Now reflect on your life today knowing that these moments happened.*

2. Send a thankful message to 3 people each Monday

Start the week in a positive and appreciative frame of mind by sending a text, email or letter, or make a phone call, to three people who helped you in some way, big or small. They might be your parents, friends, work colleagues. You can thank them for helping you in a big way or you can thank them for simply being there when you needed them.

Who are 3 people you can thank right now?

_____

_____

3. At night-time list 5 good things that happened that day

Finish each day by recording five good things that occurred. They could be as simple as befriending someone on the train, having a coffee with a workmate, finishing a report, enjoying a Pilates class, or being bowled over by your dog when you walked through the door of your home. It allows you to end the day with feelings of gratitude and sets you up for a wonderful night's sleep. This will be your Gratitude Diary, your book of smiles, which you can always go to if you need a gentle reminder about the good things in your life.

What are 5 things that happened today that you are grateful for?

_____

_____

4. In the morning list 5 things in your life you are thankful for

Start the day by thinking about all the good things in your present life. You may like to do it in bed before going to the bathroom or at the breakfast table. It lets you start your day from a position of strength and vitality (glass half-full approach), as opposed to a position of weakness or dread (glass half-empty). Don't focus on the pile of work waiting for you at the office or the traffic jams you'll likely encounter. Instead fill your mind with warm happy thoughts about your family, your health, your exercise regime.

What are 5 things in your life that you are grateful for?

_____

_____

5. Remember to thank the 'little' people

There are so many people who drift through our lives making our days that much easier whom we forget to thank properly. People like our hairdresser, the tram conductor, the supermarket cashier, the street sweeper, the restaurant waiter, the police officer walking the beat, the university lecturer or administrator. All these people have the same emotions as us and they hunger for the same recognition and acknowledgement as we do. Make their day by giving them a big cheesy smile and telling them how much you appreciate their efforts.

Who are 3 'little' people you are going to thank today?

_____

_____

6. Channel your gratitude into acts of contribution

Challenge yourself by committing some time towards weekly or monthly volunteer work for a charity or cause important to you. You will be amazed at how much you get back from the experience.

7. Role-model gratitude to children

Grab every chance you get to either demonstrate an act of gratitude or involve youngsters in a goodwill project. Some suggestions include: work gratitude into daily conversation around the family home; ask your son to help you make soup for a sick neighbor; have you and your daughter stand up on the train for an elderly couple; get the family to spring clean the bedroom closets for unused clothes for the Salvation Army; involve the family in writing thank-you notes and in recognizing each person's household weekly duties; commit the whole family to the annual community clean-up day; during holidays, and particularly the festive season, draw attention to what the children have, and not on what they don't have or want.

Extra Resources

Autry, J. A. (2012). *Choosing gratitude: Learning to love the life you have.*

Macon, GA: Smyth & Helwys.

DeMoss, N. L. (2011*). Choosing gratitude: Your journey to joy*. Chicago, IL: Moody Publishers.

Rubin, G. (2011). *The happiness project one-sentence journal: A five-year record*. Potter Style.

<u>Practice Happiness 18</u>

Reignite your curiosity of the world around you

Learn to:

❖ Reignite your curiosity about this amazing world
❖ See the extraordinary in the ordinary – by being a child, a tourist, a photographer, an anthropologist, an archaeologist, an adventurer, and an alien

1. Be a child

Remember how you lost yourself in simple activities as a child – watching a trail of ants on the pathway, making daisy chains, sailing leaf boats in the drains after a storm, feeling the heart beat of your dog. Do so again.

What are 3 simple activities you could do to recapture the child within you? (if you have children, involve them in your fun)

_____

_____

2. Be a tourist

Visit your local council and ask for a list of local walks, groups, attractions. Do the same thing in your nearest city and collect all the materials they give to visitors at the tourist bureau. On the weekends head off with a friend and explore your town.

3. Be a photographer

Grab a map and your camera and wander the streets. Take photos around a particular theme – flowers, people, wildlife, houses.

4. Be an anthropologist

What are some questions you would love to ask your friends or your parents about their backgrounds? Questions about their ancestors, childhood, teenage fears and dreams, current passions and dreams.

> Sit down with your mum or dad today or on the weekend and ask them questions that get at their deeper true selves. They will appreciate your interest.

5. Be an archaeologist

Rather than skim over the surface of books and articles go deep, very deep. Fully explore a significant moment in history and all of the characters, plots, and subplots within. You might find that book you've wanted to write all these years.

What is a book you would love to write? A novel, a travel book, the best gardens in the city, a family history, DIY ideas around the home, tips for owners of classic cars. Just for fun do a bit of brainstorming.

_____

_____

6. Be an adventurer

Every day set yourself the goal of doing something new – walk a different way to the shops, drive a different route to work, do a different type of exercise, eat a new food, talk to a stranger, watch a different program, read a different type of book. You are too young to be stuck in your ways.

What are 2 simple things you could do differently today to bring out the adventurer in you?

_____

_____

7. Be an alien

When talking with someone pretend you are an alien free of all the earthbound assumptions, expectations, and judgments. Listen and then paraphrase back to the person what you heard. Did you hear them correctly? This can be a real fun thing to do on a rainy day with a best friend. Be an alien.

Practice Happiness 19

Remain young at heart

Learn to:

❖ Remain young at heart
❖ Celebrate something every day
❖ Challenge expectations associated with your age

---

1. Love

Affection and companionship is the key here. Surround yourself with people who love you and who you love. And demonstrate your love for them every day with visits, phone calls, gifts, and good news.

2. Celebrate life every day

Celebrate your birthday. Celebrate good news. Celebrate the family and friends you have. Celebrate the fact that there is a whole world of people just outside your door that are potential friends. Celebrate the start of a sunny day.

Who are 5 people in your life whose birthdays you should celebrate? Write down their birthdays and how you may celebrate them.

_____

_____

3. Smile and laugh every chance you get
Children smile twenty times more than adults do each day. Get yourself in the mood by laughing. Smile at everyone you meet and then watch them smile right back at you.

4. Exercise regularly
It's all about energy. Apart from slowing down the aging process and helping with weight control one of the key benefits of physical exercise is energy. With this magical elixir the future with all of your dreams is possible.

What are 5 things you could do or do better if you had unlimited energy?

_____

_____

One of the main ingredients of remaining young at heart is being energetic. Exercise is the best way of keeping you feeling energetic. Consider making it one of your values.

5. Schedule in some children time every week

Children are the Zen Masters of imagination. Watch them at play. Turn off your iPhone and surrender to their world. Get totally caught up in what they are doing; the thrill, the fantasy, the chaos, the madness, the fun.

6. Do one spontaneous thing every day

Do something totally unexpected on the spur of the moment. Let the universe be your guide. Take in the sights and smells and sounds and wander where you will. Stop at an unknown coffee shop? Hop on a train and go to the end of the line? Visit a friend unannounced? Maybe take the car and play tourist for the morning. Whatever you do physically move and change your environment.

Grab your wallet or purse – and a dice – and just walk out the door. No plan. When you get to a junction or intersection let the dice be your guide. Assign a direction to a number, toss the dice, and follow the number that shows up. Smile at every one you meet. Have fun!

7. Have some younger friends

They will help you avoid becoming a victim of 'age-appropriate' behaviors and realize that there are no such behaviors. Pay attention to what they talk about, the trends, the clothes they wear, the shows they watch, their toys. Remember you used to be their age.

8. Challenge your expectations about age

Are we only allowed to play on the swings or dance in the street when we are with our children? Is it important that other adults see us being serious all the time? Is there a law against 50 year olds wearing jeans that hang half way down their backsides? Do fathers or grandfathers have to behave a certain way? Think about these questions and remember that you write your own rule book for your life – YOU.

What are some of the expectations associated with your age group that you're having second thoughts about?

_____

_____

9. Keep traveling as long as you can

Not only does traveling expose us to unfamiliar sights and sounds but it also opens a porthole to new ways of thinking and encourages us to reflect on our own perspective. Different countries mean different senses of humor, different values, and different beliefs. Get out there and give those assumptions and stereotypes of yours a real good shake-up.

10. Keep surprising yourself

Experiment with different types of music, movies, exercise, foods, restaurants, sports, and books. Instead of mainstream Hollywood-type movies try watching a few foreign films. Spice up your usual gym session with a few Pilates classes and Zumba workouts. Have breakfast at the hippest coffee bar downtown. Learn a new language. Never tried skydiving? And you've always wondered what it must feel like? Do it!

What are 3 'out there' activities on your bucket list that you still want to do? Commit yourself to a deadline with each. Here. Now.

_____

_____

```
┌─────────────────────────────────────────────────┐
│                Practice Happiness 20              │
│          The best things in life are moments      │
│                                                   │
│                    Learn to:                      │
│      ❖ Better understand your happy moments       │
│      ❖ Better savor your happy moments            │
│      ❖ Enjoy a greater number of special moments  │
│                                                   │
└─────────────────────────────────────────────────┘
```

1. Keep a Happy Moments Diary

This activity will help you better understand and replicate the moments that make you happy. Every few days keep a record of any memorable happy moments. For each moment think about the specific characteristics of *what made the moment so memorable*. Who was involved? Where were you? Was achieving a goal or meeting an expectation involved? How did the moment align with your values?

_____

_____

2. Fully surrender to the moment

To truly savor your future moments try using all your senses. At the same time avoid unnecessary distractions (feeling the need to take photos, having future-oriented thoughts, multitasking) and allow yourself to simply focus on one thing at a time – the moment.

3. Search your feelings

Slow down and smell the roses. When you are constantly busy you miss out on connecting with your feelings. And it is your feelings that are the central ingredient of special moments. So the next time you are enjoying a special moment listen to your feelings.

4. Enjoy a greater number of special moments

After spending time on the previous activities you will be able to recognize key characteristics common to your past special moments. Certain values, senses, places, events, people, and ambitions will stand out. Write down the common characteristics here.

_____

_____

Incorporate these elements into your life on a more regular basis to experience more happy moments in the future.

The next time you are hugging your partner notice each of your senses at play – your partner's smell, the contours of their body, the texture of their clothes, feel the way their body moves each time they breathe, and hear each of their breaths.

Practice Happiness 21

Savor the moment by practicing mindfulness

Learn to:

- ❖ Be more relaxed
- ❖ Keep your mind free of judgments
- ❖ Stay in the present by keeping your thoughts aligned with your behaviors
- ❖ Become a more effective listener

---

1. Mindful observation

Focus on watching something for one minute. You could visually explore something in nature such as a cloud, a bird, a trail of ants, or a flower. Let any intrusive thoughts fall away as you concentrate on the shape, texture, and smell of the object. Watching children at play is another wonderful activity here. Imagine yourself in the body of the child and feel the natural feelings of happiness as you skip and swing and laugh.

2. One-minute breathing
For one minute solely focus on your breathing. There are to be no other distractions. Inhale through your nose slowly for a count of five and then exhale from your mouth slowly for a count of five. With every inhalation imagine your body filling up with positive energy. This is a great activity to help centre and relax yourself. Try it when stuck in a traffic jam or when you first hop onto a train, arrive at your office, or take a seat at the cinema.

3. Mindful eating
Enjoy a meal with no distractions present – no TV, iPad, Smartphone, book, music, or talking. Chew food on both sides of your mouth, distinguish the individual ingredients by tastes and textures, smell the food, completely finish swallowing the food you are eating before taking another mouthful, watch the way you hold your cutlery and the way you cut the food. Repeat the exercise when you have company – you are not to speak when you have food in your mouth, and you are not to leave the table until you have finished swallowing your last mouthful of food.

4. Mindful reading
Begin by finding a quiet place where you won't be distracted. When reading, put yourself in the story – with each sentence visualize the setting, the characters, the time of day, the smells, the sounds of people talking. This takes practice. Every so often you will find your thoughts wandering about your daily concerns. When this happens, stop, reread the last sentence, and continue.

5. Other mindful activities you can do at home

- When showering, hold the soap in your non-dominant hand and feel the contours of your body.
- When brushing your teeth, try using your non-dominant hand.
- When washing dishes, clean each item separately while feeling its shape. In fact, any regular routine that you normally pay little attention to is a wonderful opportunity to practice mindfulness.
- Also, when holding your pet, feel it breathing, smell its fur, wonder at its thoughts and emotions.
- When listening to music, listen for and identify each of the individual instruments. Hear the pauses in the music. Hear when the singer inhales. Avoid judging the genre of music or the singer.

To better incorporate mindfulness into your daily life download one of the mindfulness phone apps. One example is the '*mindfulness gong*' app on your phone – every time you hear the gong practice a mindfulness activity such as one-minute breathing, listening to music, or doing a scan of your body posture.

6. Mindful walking

When walking, put all of your concentration into the present moment. Do not take an iPod or a Smartphone with you. This is time you spend with yourself. Listen to your body's joints, feel the rustle of your clothes against your skin, feel the beads of sweat and taste your saliva, become aware of your breathing, feel your muscles flexing and contracting, feel the pressure of your feet on the ground, feel the wind in your hair and the warmth of sunlight, hear the sounds of birds and the wind in the trees.

7. Mindful driving

You don't need to drive an MGB Roadster to enjoy this activity. Wind down (that means 'lower' for people who bought a car made in the 21st century) the windows in your car. As you drive along, listen for birds and people talking. Feel the gear changes and the acceleration of the car when you take off from the lights. Avoid judging the behaviors of other drivers.

This mindful body scan can help you get to sleep by calming your mind and relaxing your body.

- Begin by doing the one-minute breathing activity.
- Then, starting at the top of your head, imagine a laser beam slowly passing down the length of your body. As the laser beam travels become aware of the weight of various body parts against the mattress (e.g. back of the head, shoulders, lower back, buttocks, calves).
- Repeat the exercise, but this time as the laser passes along, first flex your muscles separately for 3 seconds, and then relax the same muscles (e.g. forehead, mouth, shoulders, buttocks, quadriceps, calves).
- Finish by focusing on your breathing.....Nighty night!

8. Mindfulness without judgment

This is such a key component of mindfulness because when you are passing judgments in your mind (about a person's behavior or their choice of clothes and friends, about who caused a door to slam, about a driver who cut you off, and so on) you are not fully in the present moment. When you do this you have started thinking about the past (perhaps comparing yourself to others) or the future (worrying about the possible consequences of an action). And as soon as you make judgments emotions are triggered. So, to prevent the rise of negative emotions such as anxiety and regret avoid making judgments and stay in the present.

9. Listen mindfully

This is where you get to put into practice your skills in mindfulness. When involved in a conversation, listen carefully to what the person is saying to you – hear the words, watch their body movements, and feel their emotions. Most importantly, listen without judgment. As they are talking resist the urge to interrupt with your own opinions or comments. Focus on what *they want*, not on what you want. Then, to acknowledge them and to check that you have heard them correctly, paraphrase what they said back to them.

10. Take control of the chattering monkey

You need to set present-oriented thinking as your default position of thinking. If your thoughts stray to the future or to the past – the chattering monkey – gently bring them back to the activity you are doing and refocus on your senses. I find meditation to be a wonderful way to help develop this discipline. Your goal is to be thinking about what you are doing at a particular moment – eating, riding a bike, driving, running, listening to a friend, reading, giving a presentation, massaging your partner. Once again, whenever you notice your concentration begin to waver bring your thoughts back to the task at hand. Practice this again and again and again. To make the most of each day your thoughts and your body must be in synch, both in the present.

Extra Resources

Gunaratana, B. H. (2011). *Mindfulness in plain English: 20th anniversary edition.* Somerville, MASS: Wisdom Publications.

Williams, M., Penman, D. (2012). *Mindfulness: An eight-week plan for finding peace in a frantic world.* Emmaus, PA: Rodale.

<u>Practice Happiness 22</u>

Breathing is the easiest way to stay in the present

Learn to:

❖ Identify your own breathing style

❖ Breathe properly for optimal health

❖ Feel less stressed through proper breathing

❖ Realize that you mimic others' breathing patterns

1. Check your breathing style

First, you need to check whether you are using diaphragmatic breathing or not.

- Lie down on your bed or on the lounge room floor and place one hand on your chest and place the other hand on your abdomen, just above your belly button.

- Have both palms facing down.

- Breathe the way you normally do and notice which hand moves the most, the chest hand or the abdominal hand. When you are breathing correctly and are using your diaphragm the hand on your abdomen will be moving and the hand on your chest will be virtually still.

- When your chest hand is moving more than your abdominal hand, you are breathing mainly with your chest. This indicates shallow breathing.

- Get into the habit of checking your breathing at regular intervals –

in the car at the traffic jam, at your computer desk, standing in line at the bank.

2. How to breathe properly using diaphragmatic breathing

Follow these steps to breathe diaphragmatically.

- Lie down or sit down. Loosen any tight clothing and consider removing your shoes and glasses.
- Once again, place one hand on your chest, the other hand on your abdomen.
- Focus on your breathing. Inhale through your nose slowly for a count of 4 seconds (1, 2, 3, 4). When you inhale imagine your lungs as balloons filling up with air. Feel your chest widening slightly, your diaphragm pulling your chest cavity down, and your belly button pulling away from your spine.
- Then exhale slowly through your mouth for a count of 4 seconds (1, 2, 3, 4). When you exhale imagine the balloons deflating and feel your belly button backing in towards your spine as you push the air out of your lungs.
- Continue this process. This will give you 7-8 breaths per minute. Avoid taking fast deep breaths. Continue practicing slow deep breaths.

3. Set aside a time each day to practice deep breathing

This could be part of your daily meditation session. Or possibly when you first wake up and are thinking your gratitude thoughts. Or maybe when you hop into bed at night and are reflecting on your accomplishments for the day – a great way to send you off to sleep. Practice taking 10 deep breaths. You could also try using an app on your computer or on your iPhone such as *BreathPacer*.

4. Take deep breaths when you feel anxious

We've all been told to count to 10 when feeling anxious, when involved in an argument, or before making an important decision. It gives us a short time-out and allows us a moment to put whatever is bothering us into perspective. Very useful advice but it's only half the story. Here's the full story:

- While counting to 10 take in big breaths and then imagine exhaling all the negativity and the muscle tension from your body.

- Quickly scan your body from head to toe to check that there is no tightness remaining in your muscles. If there is, take further deep breaths and with every exhalation allow your muscles to loosen and become heavy.

- Finally, imagine positive energy filling up your body every time you inhale.

One of the best ways to stay in the present moment and to develop the habit of taking slow deep breaths is to inhale scents around you – when you walk through the perfumery at a department store, when passing a barbeque at a park, filling up at the petrol station, or when hanging out at the local coffee shop. Even less-than pleasant smells can help you to refocus on the now.

5. Be conscious of your breath throughout the day

Pay attention to your breathing rate when you are happy, sad, frustrated, excited, or feeling numb. You will probably notice that you breathe slowly and calmly when happy and quickly when angry. Whenever you notice a different emotion, assess your breathing rate and then return your breathing rate to its default factory setting. This exercise will help you, not only become more aware of your emotions during the day, but also control your emotions. Your emotions and your breathing rate are directly linked. Control one, control the other.

6. Breathe deeply to improve your posture

When sitting at your desk or standing in a queue practice breathing deeply and watch how you naturally straighten up. Filling your lungs encourages you to straighten your spine and sit or stand taller.

7. Appreciate the other physical benefits of slow deep breathing

Carbon dioxide is a natural toxic waste produced by the body's metabolic processes. It is transferred from the blood to our lungs and we expel it when we breathe. Up to 70 percent of toxins are released from the body in this way. Therefore, for optimal health it is vital that we breathe slowly and deeply consistently. Some of the other benefits of deep breathing include relieving pain, improving digestion, stimulating the lymphatic system, and increasing cardiovascular capacity.

Wherever you are right now, sit up straight and practice slow deep breathing for 2 minutes. As you do this become conscious of all your senses – feel your various body parts contacting the chair and the floor, smell the air, hear your breathing, taste the saliva in your mouth.

8. Be aware that you mimic other peoples' breathing patterns

We tend to mimic each other's breathing patterns particularly when we are in a group situation. This is why we pick up another person's tension so easily (*also see the story on Secondhand Stress in Section 2*). University students intuitively know this as they plug into the music on their iPhone outside exam venues rather than be infected by everyone else's feelings of anxiety. So when in a group monitor your own breathing rate and your emotions.

Extra Resources

Brown, R. P., & Gerbarg, P. L. (2012). *The healing power of the breath: Simple techniques to reduce stress and anxiety, enhance concentration, and balance your emotions.* Boston, MASS: ShamBhala Publications.

Strom, M. (2007). *Max Strom: Learn to breathe.* DVD.

Weil, A. (1999). *Breathing: The master key to self healing (the self healing series).* Audio CD. Sounds True.

Practice Happiness 23
Live each day as if it could be your last

Learn to:
❖ Imagine whether you would live differently if there were no guarantees about your future
❖ Imagine your likely future if you continue living as you are now
❖ See that the perfect time to grab that opportunity is always now
❖ Laugh more every day

---

1. What if you were told that *any day* could be your last?
How would you live your life differently? Imagine it in your mind. Notice how it forces you to bring your thinking back in time to the present. This can be a very powerful exercise which can dramatically alter your perception of time.

So what would you do differently this week if you knew that any day could be your last? (e.g. take that short driving trip you've been putting off, go for a walk every day instead of every second day, ring up the girl next door you've had your eye on for some time, start that community college course you've been deliberating about for months.)

2. What future awaits you if you continue living the way you are now?

This activity requires real insight and honesty. If you continue to live the way you are currently living – absorbed in future or past-oriented thinking – what is your likely future? What type of person will you become? What type of person *are* you becoming? Your likely partner? Your likely job prospects? Your likely financial status? And keep in mind that the longer you wait to change your lifestyle and mode of thinking certain factors will start to weigh against you, such as your advancing age, a diminishing likelihood to take risks, the burden of mounting regrets, finding it harder to attract a partner. All of this equates into powerful incentives to change your life today.

3. Stop waiting for the perfect time to arrive

We are pretty good at coming up with a host of reasons for not doing things now. We're either too young or too old or too busy or too broke or too tired. When presented with an opportunity our first thought is often, "If only he had asked me tomorrow." But then tomorrow arrives and the opportunity has passed, or something actually does arise that we could never have foreseen, or we come up with some other excuse. When we consistently do this, not only do we miss out on opportunities in the present, but we also lose the opportunity to develop momentum and to make acting in the moment a habit. Opportunities arise when they are ready, not when we are ready. So grab those opportunities now and trust in yourself.

4. The perfect time is NOW

When trying to decide whether to make a lifestyle change or capitalize on an opportunity make a list of all the things in your favor – support of loved ones, your good health, your vitality and energy, your self-confidence, your maturity, perhaps your strong financial base, your travel and worldly experience, the belief the other person must have had in you to tell you about the opportunity, your spiritual faith.

What is an opportunity currently on your mind? Write down all the things in your favor of making it a success.

_____

_____

As they say, laughter is the best medicine. It's a great workout for the heart, fills you with happiness, and attracts people like bees to honey. Here are some tips for laughing more.

- Train yourself to smile wherever you go, whatever you're doing. You'll feel instantly better and you'll see how contagious it is with strangers.

- Practice laughing every day in the familiar surroundings of your home when showering, cooking, listening to your favorite music, playing with your dog, or tickling your partner.

- Adopt a regular diet of humorous films, books, and TV shows that make you feel happy about yourself and the world.

- Surround yourself with funny or upbeat people who bring out your lighter side.

- Don't take yourself so seriously. When you stuff up, pause, and then laugh. You'll be in a much better frame of mind to return to the task at hand.

Time for a giggle.

A young soldier and his commanding officer got on a train together. The only available seats were across from an attractive young woman traveling with her grandmother. The soldier and the young woman kept eyeing one another; it was obvious they were attracted to one another.

Suddenly the train went into a tunnel and the car became pitch black. Immediately two sounds were heard: the "smack" of a kiss, and the "whack" of a slap across the face.

The grandmother thought, "I can't believe he kissed my granddaughter, but I'm glad she gave him the slap he deserved." The commanding officer thought, "I don't blame the boy for kissing the girl, but it's a shame that she missed his face and slapped me instead." The young girl thought, "I'm glad he kissed me, but I wish my grandmother hadn't slapped him for doing it."

And as the train emerged from the tunnel into sunlight, the soldier couldn't keep the smile off his face. He had just grabbed the opportunity to kiss a beautiful girl and slap his commanding officer and had gotten away with both!

Extra Resources

Goodheart, A. (1994). *Laughter therapy: How to laugh about everything in your life that isn't really funny.* Santa Barbara, CALIF: Less Stress Press.

Klein, A. (1989). *The healing power of humor.* New York, NY: Putnam.

Practice Happiness 24

Clean out your emotional cupboards

Learn to:

❖ Forgive yourself for any past wrongs
❖ Let go of grudges against others
❖ Realize that you are responsible for your own emotional baggage
❖ Spring clean any emotional baggage in your relationships

---

1. Learn to forgive yourself

Forgiving yourself can be much harder than forgiving someone else. But if you are to release yourself from the events of your past and move forward with hope and purpose then you must forgive yourself. Here are some suggestions for achieving this:

- Practice self-acceptance. This means that you accept yourself and your faults. None of us are perfect. Expecting yourself to be perfect is unrealistic and will only set you up for future disappointments. So, love yourself as you are but focus on forgiving yourself for specific behaviors that you feel bad about.

- Let go of other people's expectations for you. Sometimes we berate ourselves for not living up to our parents' or our partner's expectations. Remember that it is your life and your purpose that matters, not theirs. Refuse to take ownership of their goals for your life.

- Understand that self-forgiveness does not mean forgetting or condoning what you did. Acknowledge your past wrong, learn from it, and then move forward.

- Appreciate the importance of self-forgiveness. Forgiving yourself will relieve you of destructive feelings like vulnerability, guilt, and sadness, and will replace them with the positive feelings of self-compassion, self-improvement, and hope for the future.

- Forgiving yourself will allow you to become a healthier and happier version of you which will help enrich both the quality of your life and the relationships you have with others.

2. Let go of grudges and resentment against others

Perhaps your partner had an affair, a colleague claimed credit for your work, a friend double-crossed you behind your back, or your father criticized you in front of his friends. In all these cases it wouldn't be unreasonable for you to feel angry and bitter. Someone you love or trusted has hurt you. However, if you don't practice forgiveness, the negative emotions will fester, not only damaging your relationship with the other person, but depriving *yourself* of love and peace. Once you make the conscious decision to forgive your feelings of bitterness will gradually be replaced by feelings of compassion, kindness, and peace. And you will be able to regain control of your life and move forward.

Are you holding a grudge against anyone at the moment? Is it benefiting you? Imagine now how you would feel letting go of the grudge and forgiving the person.

_____

_____

Now that you've identified an unresolved grudge take the next step – make a commitment to see the person before the week is out to resolve the matter. Remain focused on how this will benefit both the friendship and your own happiness.

3. Avoid judging others

Accept people as they are. We are all different and each of us brings something unique to the world. When we judge the clothing, behaviors, cars, opinions of others we are setting ourselves up as the golden standard. We do this because of our own insecurities. By appreciating our own uniqueness, rather than comparing ourselves to others, we will feel more content and at peace within ourselves and will better appreciate the uniqueness of others.

4. Remember that you are responsible for your own emotional baggage

Every day we choose how happy or how sad we want to be – whether we want to be rolling around in the emotional muck of our past, or enjoying the present and enthusiastically anticipating the future. The best we can do is learn from the hurts of the past, forgive ourselves and others for things that may have been done or said, and then embrace the present wholeheartedly and with passion.

5. Do a regular stock take of all the good things in your life

This will help you stop fixating on the one or two bad things that are happening and make you realize how good your life is overall. Be happy with what IS now. Be happy with what you have now. Be happy with who you are now. And know that the grass is greener on YOUR side of the fence. Why? Because that's where you are!

6. Regularly spring clean any emotional baggage in your relationship

Set aside a time every day for being with your partner without distractions. Set guidelines for non-judgmental listening and then permit each other to talk about anything. You might share a joyful experience from work, you might air a grievance you have with your partner about household duties, or you might want to discuss your child's school report card. Get it out there. Make sure that each partner accepts responsibility for the solution of any problem discussed. Both parties must be committed to resolving the issue.

Is there any emotional baggage in your relationship you need to air and discard? Put it down on paper and then share it with your partner.

---

7. Consider talking to someone else

It could be a close friend but preferably a counselor, psychologist, or life coach, who is fluent in the principles of non-judgmental listening and reflective listening. This is Pilates for the heart where you offload your emotional baggage and think carefully about your present and future emotional goals.

Extra Resources

Enright, R. D. (2001). *Forgiveness is a choice: A step-by-step process for resolving anger and restoring hope.* Washington, DC: APA LifeTools.

Jakes, T. D. (2013). *Let it go: Forgive so you can be forgiven.* New York, NY: Atria Books.

Practice Happiness 25
You don't need more stuff to be happy

Learn to:
❖ Check if having more things aligns with your life purpose and values
❖ Ask yourself these questions when you feel the urge to buy something
❖ Savor experiences that are free or cost very little

---

1. Reestablish your purpose

One of the most important things you can do to both help combat an addiction to always wanting more stuff and to satisfy any follow-on feelings of emptiness is to reestablish your life purpose. While acquiring possessions is a fleeting pleasure, focusing on your purpose for living is enduring.

Write down your life purpose and ponder whether it conflicts with wanting to accumulate more stuff.

_____

_____

2. Consider doing more volunteer work

This goes hand-in-hand with reestablishing your life purpose and making your life more meaningful. Helping others takes your mind off yourself and your own needs. It will also help you appreciate the blessings in your life and bear witness that many people with much less than yourself are quite happy.

3. Reassess your values and your goals

Reconnect with your values and your goals discussed in Step 1. Is money high on your value list? Is wanting more things high on your value list? If so, you may want to reassess your value hierarchy.

_____

_____

What meaningful goals do you currently have in your life to keep you engaged in the present? Write them down.

_____

_____

Is wanting to buy more stuff a way of distracting yourself from a lack of meaningful goals in your life? *You may need to develop more inspiring goals.*

4. Take responsibility for your feelings of happiness

Refrain from saying "I will be happy when…" Realize that you can be happy any time you want. Like right NOW. Appreciate that your feelings of happiness do not have to be dependent upon accumulating possessions. Reexamine your Gratitude Diary to remind you of the many non-material things in your life you have to be grateful for.

5. Do a stock take of your happiest moments

Recall 10 of your happiest moments.

_____

_____

Were they when you were alone with certain possessions or were they when you were with other people or achieving a personal goal?
(Your happiest moments probably occurred when you were fully engaged in the present in activities such as watching a sunset with your partner, picnicking with friends, laughing at the antics of your pet dog, holding your newly-born child, watching your son's graduation ceremony, receiving the news of your promotion.)

6. Savor everyday experiences that are free or cost very little

When we pay too much attention to money, we begin to value things simply because of their cost. So, spend time watching glorious sunsets or visit an observatory to marvel at the stars in the night sky. Enjoy that simple coffee with a friend, the walk along the beachfront, the birds cooing in the trees.

Brainstorm enjoyable things you can do either by yourself or with friends that cost very little. (This can be a fun activity to do with your friends.)

_____

_____

7. Develop strategies to help you stop buying stuff

Start thinking of strategies to help you resist the urge to open your wallet or purse. If you have to, avoid window-shopping and, maybe, leave your credit cards and most of your cash at home. Tell your friends of your intention to cut back on needless purchases and solicit their help.

When you suddenly feel the urge to buy something stop and ask yourself:
- Is this thing really better than the things I already have?
- What can I do with this thing that I can't do with my other possessions?
- Do I really need it?
- How is it going to add value to my life?
- How often can I honestly see myself using it each day or each week?
- What will become of my other possessions that this thing is replacing?

 Give these questions a road test as soon as possible. Organize a shopping expedition with one of your friends who understands your desire to buy less unnecessary stuff. Every time either one of you becomes spellbound by an item in the store answer each of the questions.

Extra Resources

Morgenstern, J. (2009). *Shed your stuff, change your life: A four step guide to getting unstuck.* New York, NY: Fireside.

Palaian, S. (2009). *Spent: Break the buying obsession and discover your true worth.* Center City, MINN: Hazelden.

Step

4

Live a Fully Connected Life

Enjoy more meaningful
and fulfilling relationships

In this step

How to enjoy more effective conversations

*

Look for opportunities to practice the Golden Rule every day

*

Speak to be heard and speak to be felt

*

Celebrate humanity by talking with strangers every day

*

Compliment a stranger makes you both feel good instantly

*

Become known as a person who always spreads good news

*

Perform random acts of kindness every day

*

How to celebrate our similarities and our differences

*

Focus on understanding another before being understood

*

Look for the positive intention behind a person's behavior

Practice Happiness 26

E-Messages are no substitution for face-to-face conversations

Learn to:

❖ Lay down rules and boundaries at the start of important conversations

❖ Practice the most important rule for maintaining a conversation

❖ Demonstrate effective conversation skills to your children

---

1. Adopt a body posture that invites conversation

Walking around with head bowed to a screen or being hunched over a laptop does nothing to encourage people to want to interact with you. Give yourself the opportunity to meet more people and to further develop your conversation skills by looking up and seeking eye contact when going about your daily business. And when talking with someone don't fidget or keep glancing towards your tablet – stay focused on the other person. Give them your full attention and in time they will start to mirror your behaviors.

2. Disable and put away your devices during conversations

At the start of a conversation, if you think it's necessary, lay down a few rules and boundaries. For example, all devices must be turned off and placed out of sight. Let the other person know the reasons for doing these things – shows respect for each other, allows each party to concentrate on the topic at hand, lessens the chances of miscommunication, and gives each person the opportunity to clarify issues with follow-up questions.

3. Set regular times for conversation with your loved ones

The main culprits for the break-up of couples today are

miscommunication and insufficient communication. Couples are not communicating enough and when they do communicate it is not effective or sufficiently satisfying for both parties. One way to address this is to schedule a regular time, perhaps each day, for some quality uninterrupted conversation. There doesn't have to be an agenda. It's simply time to be with your partner without any distractions or time commitments. These are the moments when we reveal ourselves and truly get to really understand each other.

When during the day or week do you think would be a good time for regular uninterrupted conversation with your partner? Where would you like this to happen? (at home, which room; away from home) Are there any particular topics you would like to discuss with your partner during these sessions? Share these ideas with your partner.

_____

_____

4. Decide on device-free zones

As a parent, let family members know which rooms in the home (maybe the dining room and kitchen), times (when visitors drop in or during meal times), and away-from-home places (other people's homes and at church) are off-limits for using devices.

What times and what places would you like to designate as device-free zones for your family or with your partner? Discuss your ideas with them.

_____

_____

5. Demonstrate the value of conversation to your children

Children need to see their parents role modeling effective conversation skills including: their regularity and normalcy, clearly stating the agenda (if any) of a discussion, direct eye contact, putting away any distracting devices, muting TVs, respectful listening, some degree of paraphrasing to gauge understanding, intelligent questioning, and appropriate body language.

When trying to maintain a conversation remember the most important rule. Talk about them, not about yourself. Whenever you feel the conversation begin to drag and falter focus on the other person's needs instead of your own. The following questions always hit the spot:

- "What did you wish to talk about?"
- "What things are keeping you busy at the moment?"
- "What's been the highlight of your past week?"
- "What are you looking forward to doing in the near future?"
- "Is there anything I can help you with?"

6. Refuse to be short-changed on conversation

When someone replies to your question with the word, "Whatever ..." ask them to explain what they mean. You can choose not to accept one-word answers or one-syllable grunts. Our cave-dwelling days are long past and one of the key conditions of a modern conversation is respect for all parties. Lay down the ground rules early on about which words and types of sentences are not acceptable in any conversation with you.

What are the words and sentences you find unacceptable in a conversation?

_____

_____

7. Tell the person how much you value your conversations with them

Make sure you express your gratitude to the person for giving up their time for a face-to-face conversation. And let them know how you benefited as well. Doing these simple things will go a long way to guaranteeing that this person will want to have future conversations with you. We all like to be appreciated.

The next time you get together with a friend who you know is a bit tech-obsessive suggest that both of you disable your devices. Then gauge the quality of your conversation free of disruptions.

Extra Resources

Shepherd, M. (2005). *The art of civilized conversation: A guide to expressing yourself with style and grace.* New York, NY: Broadway Books.

Smith, D., & Smith, B. (2003). *Conversation with character: Teaching the art of conversation, from "hello" to "farewell."* Joelton, TN: Sweet Home Press.

Practice Happiness 27
Remember the Golden Rule

Learn to:
❖ Look for opportunities to help others
❖ Choose to say nice things to people
❖ Own up to your mistakes and practice self-compassion
❖ Role-model the Golden Rule to children

---

1. Look for opportunities to help others

Simple things you can do every day such as helping elderly people cross the street, opening the door for someone else, giving up your bus seat, letting someone else buy the last muffin, offering to take a photo of a couple with their camera, helping tourists with directions, donating blood, allowing a person to hop into your traffic lane, offering a drink to charity collectors who visit your home, helping return the bins to the back of your block of units after rubbish collection day.

2. Say nice things to people

This is an extension of my mother's rule, "If you have nothing nice to say then say nothing." You want to hear good news and so do they. Say things that will make the other person happy – compliment them, find a positive thing to say about the weather, talk about personal or family successes, ask about their future holiday plans.

3. Compliment people

Find something to compliment people on such as their choice of clothes, their smile, their engaging laughter, their energy, their kindness, their choice of pet, the book they are reading.

What compliment could you give right now to each of the 10 closest people in your life?

_____

_____

4. Listen to others
When listening to people clear your mind of judgments and expectations. If they want solutions to their problems they will ask you for them, otherwise just listen. Listen to them the way you would want them to listen to you.

5. Look for opportunities to role-model the Golden Rule for children
When youngsters are nearby make that extra effort to pick up that litter, to say hello to their parents, to compliment them on their behaviors, to help their father lift that box into the car, to open the door for them.

What things are you or could you be doing to role-model the Golden Rule for your own children?

_____

_____

6. Admit mistakes
A key component of the Golden Rule is compassion and being able to say you are sorry and to admit when you are wrong. You would want others to do the same.

7. Forgive others
Pride is the enemy of compassion. Even if you feel the other person was at fault the relationship cannot move forward until you forgive each other. Look for the positive intention behind the person's behavior and consider the hardships they may have been dealing with

themselves. Surely you would want them to give you the benefit of the doubt as well.

8. Practice self-compassion

Show yourself some compassion by challenging the validity of your beliefs and expectations. Tell yourself that you deserve to be loved and be able to love. You deserve to be happy. You deserve to be surrounded by nice people. You are allowed to make mistakes. You are not defined by your mistakes. You are entitled to follow your own dreams. Practice being your own best friend. Be kind to yourself. And remember that you are not alone – we all have fears just as we all have dreams.

For the next 2 days you are not allowed to berate yourself, no matter what the circumstances. You have to *talk yourself UP*. The way to do this is by looking for the learning experience, being your own cheer leader, and focusing on your progress instead of the end-goal.

Practice Happiness 28

Celebrate humanity by talking with strangers every day

Learn to:
- ❖ Give people the best of yourself
- ❖ Speak to be heard and speak to be felt
- ❖ Practice your conversation skills everyday
- ❖ Compliment strangers whenever possible

---

1. Before talking with strangers do this

Before you charge off and start chatting with every one you meet on the street give yourself a quick enthusiasm-for-life top-up by affirming how thankful you are for the simple things you have in your life each day – being healthy, having food in the fridge, owning a car, having people in your life who love you, having the choice to design your own life. Why wait till national holidays come along before allowing yourself to feel totally exhilarated and excited about life? Make every day a national celebration day. Your enthusiasm will quickly infect others.

2. Speak to be heard and speak to be felt

My father was my role model here. He had the ability to capture a stranger's heart in seconds by addressing them with his entire being. No whispered hellos, no "whatever"s, no greetings on the run. When he spoke to someone they heard him AND they felt him. He left them with a feeling as well as a message. This is what he did – *with his chest facing the person he was going to talk to, he looked them right in the eyes, and in a strong voice said hello with a smile.*

The next time you say hello to somebody – whether it's a stranger on the train or a person working in your office – try my father's method. You will find the person you address wanting to mirror your own body language.

3. Strangers are simply friends you haven't met yet

The number one reason why people are reluctant to talk to strangers is that they think that the stranger will think less of them somehow and reject them. This is mindreading at its very worst. Remember that we are all human and therefore have the same doubts, fears, hopes, and dreams. We all want to be liked and respected and accepted for whom we are. And we all want friends. Knowing this should give you the confidence to initiate conversations. However, the substance of your words has to be positive, complimentary, and uplifting.

4. Developing your stranger conversation skills

Although you cross paths with strangers countless times every day there are certain environments that lend themselves to more successful encounters, at least in the beginning when you are practicing your conversation skills. I am referring to the places where you see the same people even though you may have never shared a conversation with them. Such as the receptionists at your doctor's clinic, the cashiers at the local supermarket, the newspaper vendor down the road, and the attendant at the nearby petrol station. Once you feel more confident at starting conversations you can progress to talking with complete strangers such as passers-by on the street, people in queues, a man washing his car in the driveway, a woman walking her dog, or someone sitting next to you on the bus.

Who are 5 people you see regularly but rarely, if ever, share a conversation with? What can you say to them the next time you see them that is positive and uplifting?

_____

_____

Think about how much it will brighten their day and yours too.

5. Say nice things to strangers

Everyone prefers to hear good news rather than tales of woe. We hear enough bad news through the media. So if you wish to stand out and truly make a good impression, share a happy or uplifting story to raise a person's spirits. Probably the only reason to volunteer unhappy tales to a stranger is if you are attempting to display empathy for their situation. And even so, at a later point try to conclude the conversation on a positive note, either by suggesting possible solutions or by praising their efforts for handling things so well.

6. Compliment strangers

This is one of the best, if not the best, ways to begin a friendship. And what a simple thing it is to do. Compliments might be about how well they look, how energetic they are, the wonderful smile on their face, their infectious laugh, the dedication they must have to do their job, the great job they are doing bringing up their kids, their ability to listen. Giving a compliment helps gain trust and bolsters a person's self-esteem.

Practice Happiness 29
When you've got good news spread it around

Learn to:
❖   Listen for good news, not bad news
❖   Avoid spreading bad news
❖   Spread good news everyday
❖   Encourage others to offer good news

---

1. Listen for good news, not bad news

This takes awareness and willpower. It's your choice what thoughts you allow into your head. They can be empowering feel-good thoughts that inspire you to embrace the world or they can be limiting demoralizing thoughts that sap your energy and spirit. So choose carefully the type of media reports you watch, the books you read, and the friends you listen to.

2. Choose not to spread bad news

When you hear bad news on the grapevine, that is, in the form of gossip or media reports, be the person who doesn't pass it on. Choose not to sensationalize or fan the flame of bad news. All it does is make people miserable and feel that they have no control over their lives. Passing on good news achieves the exact opposite making people feel happy and full of hope for the future. Become known in the office as the person who always has something nice and uplifting to say.

3. Spread good news about your great day

Tell others about the interesting people you met today, the different walk route you took, the lovely park you visited for lunch, the yummy muffin you enjoyed, the person who offered you their seat on the train. Look for good things and you'll see them all around you.

What are 5 good things that happened to you today?

_____

_____

4. Spread good news of your goal progress

Share with others any successes you have had with goals you have been working on. Example goals might include losing weight, exercising, budgeting, reducing procrastination, replacing unhealthy habits with healthier habits, making new friends or getting to bed earlier. If you don't feel that you have experienced any progress towards your goals make sure you reward yourself for *the effort* you have put in. Changing habits takes time. Cementing habits takes longer. But remember that every attempt is taking you one step closer towards your goals – and you are the person making that happen. Well done.

What goals are you working on at the moment? What progress have you made towards them?

_____

_____

5. Spread good news of your family successes

Tell others about your husband's promotion, your grandmother's surprise birthday dinner, your daughter's first ballet class, your son's goal in soccer, the family's weekend trip to the beach. And then inquire about their family successes.

6. Spread good news of your work successes

Share with others the reasons behind your salary bonus, how you instilled more fun into your more mundane daily tasks, how you have improved your time management skills allowing you to leave the office on time each day, interesting details about the new crew at work. Then inquire about their work successes.

7. Spread good news about your friend's success

Tell others about the success your friend is enjoying getting fit at the new local gym, at redoing his wardrobe, at discovering a great place to buy cheap good quality children's clothes, at receiving a message out of the blue from an old school friend on Facebook. Others can then benefit from the feelings of happiness and then be inspired to create their own success moments.

Start a conversation with a friend about a movie you saw. See how long the conversation continues before negativity creeps in (e.g. movie was awful, terrible weather, gossip, crazy car traffic). *The point is it takes effort to maintain a positive conversation.* But for the wonderful feelings of happiness it's worth it!

8. Receiving good news

Encourage others to tell you their good news by asking them, "What was the best thing that happened to you today?" Also, when someone shares with you their good news show excitement and encourage them to share further good news moments. Then you can reciprocate by sharing your own good news.

9. Receiving bad news from a friend

When a friend shares their bad news with you it's natural to want to listen to them and show compassion and comfort them. This helps them 'mourn' and come to terms with the event. It's an important and necessary part of the grieving process. However, you need to be careful of becoming bogged down in the bad news where the two of you sit around replaying the event over and over again. Dwelling excessively on bad news deadens the heart and causes us to become inward focused and lose our capacity for problem-solving. Instead, after an appropriate period of 'mourning' the unhappy event, encourage your friend to look for a silver lining or for solutions forward.

Practice Happiness 30
Look for opportunities to help people every day

Learn to:
- ❖ Practice daily random acts of kindness
- ❖ Be a cheer squad for others
- ❖ Surprise your loved ones each week

---

1. Perform daily random acts of kindness (RAK)

The principle behind performing RAK is to do good deeds to others with no thought of receiving anything in return. The good deed may be spontaneous or planned and may be performed anonymously. The goal may be to try and perform one RAK each day. The gift to the giver is the selfless joy of giving.

Some typical RAK include: paying the bill for the person in the queue or at the tollbooth behind you; making other drivers aware of the existence of parking enforcement officers; filling up others' parking meters; and topping up public laundry washing machines.

Of course, RAK do not have to involve money. They may include acts such as helping your new neighbor move into their apartment, offering to look after your sister's kids for the night, mowing your next-door neighbor's front lawn, bringing a treat to the office for your fellow workers, or helping an elderly person cross the street.

Challenge yourself to perform one RAK each day for the whole week for a particular group of people – perhaps your work colleagues, or your neighbors, or fellow commuters on your morning train. You may find that others in the group start following your example.

2. Perform random acts of kindness for yourself

Why not regularly perform RAK for yourself? Take yourself out for a movie, for dinner, for a bike ride by the river, for a picnic in the park to watch the birds, or take time out to read a book.

What are 5 RAK you performed for yourself in the last few days? If you can't think of any, then list 5 things you *will do* in the future.

_____

_____

Support others in their endeavors. Send them text messages and phone calls of encouragement. Encouraging others will also help you feel good about yourself and may strengthen your commitment to your own goals. Here are a few ways you could be a cheer squad for others.

- Give someone some useful tips for finding a job or introduce them to some of your contacts.
- Actively encourage a work colleague to go for a promotion.
- Offer to be a sounding board for a friend who wishes to share with you their goals for the year ahead.
- Encourage a friend in their weight loss efforts.
- Or you could simply cheer on passing runners in the park.

3. Commit some of your time to a charity or cause

You may like to give the gift of your time to a one-off annual charity event (e.g. Clean Up Australia Day, Smith Family Christmas Present Deliveries, Red Cross Door Knock Appeal), or you may be able to commit to a cause on a weekly basis (e.g. patrolling the beaches with the Surf Life Saving Association, providing support at a mental illness accommodation center, being a classroom helper at a primary school).

4. Each week surprise your loved ones

Have the evening meal ready when your family gets home, take your parents out to dinner on the spur of the moment, or arrive home with flowers for your partner for no particular reason. Surprise them, surprise yourself!

Extra Resources

The Editors of Conari Press. (2002). *Random acts of kindness*. San Francisco, CA: Conari Press.

Practice Happiness 31
We are all very similar and all very different

Learn to:
❖ Show more compassion for others
❖ Appreciate that you are surrounded by teachers
❖ Appreciate your own unique differences

---

1. Develop more compassion

Realize that everyone you meet, whether it's on the street or in a boardroom or at a dinner party, is wrestling with an inner struggle of their own just like you. It could be relationship issues, the demands of work, trying to decide in which direction to take their life, health issues, loneliness, financial pressures. So, be kinder than perhaps you normally are. One of life's great gifts is supporting others.

List 5 ways in which you can show greater kindness to others.

_____

_____

The Dalai Lama said, "If you want others to be happy, practice compassion. If you want to be happy, practice compassion."

2. Realize that the world is your mirror

We see this in action every day. We see it when a couple copies each other's behaviors at a dinner party, when a road rage victim's aggressive reaction is matched by the erratic driver, when a calming word from an employee placates a frustrated store customer, when a parent soothes an upset child. People react to us as we behave to them.

The next time you meet someone, either a friend or a stranger, take note of their behavior towards you. Do they smile? Do they seem open and engaging? Do they share good news or are they continuously critical of others? *Consider the possibility that their behavior and attitudes mirror your own.* Challenge yourself to get them to smile, to share with you the highlights of their week (as opposed to their lowlights), and to talk optimistically about the future (instead of wallowing in the past).

3. Develop your ability to listen

Communicating with others, particularly strangers, is a wonderful opportunity to practice the skill of non-judgmental listening. We all want to be heard and understood, not judged. When your new friend is speaking listen without judging or evaluating what they are saying. And when they finish speaking paraphrase the content of their words and their feelings back to them. Hold back your opinion until, and if, they ask for it. Otherwise, just listen.

Sometimes we bemoan the fact that people are not kind enough, generous enough, or respectful enough towards us. Knowing that the world is a mirror, is it possible that we haven't been giving enough? For the next week make a commitment to *give to others unconditionally* – give your time, give kindness, give compliments, give happiness.

4. Realize that you are surrounded by teachers

See each person you meet as a potential teacher. Constantly ask yourself, "What can I learn from this person?" Maybe you can learn something about a new food, a different sport, a book or a film, or a different way of looking at things. Maybe you will discover a strength you have that you were blind to. Maybe they can teach you tolerance and being open to the differences of others. Whatever you take away from the exchange, your world has just become a larger and much more interesting place. Of course, you have the chance to be their teacher as well – to show compassion and tolerance and positivity.

Who are 3 teachers in your life at the moment? What lessons are they teaching you?

_____

_____

Which people in your life are you a teacher for? What lessons are you teaching them?

_____

_____

5. Appreciate your own differences

Appreciating and respecting the differences of others will help you better appreciate your own unique differences. Being different is what makes you more interesting to others and to yourself. It also makes the world a much more interesting place where anything seems possible. Celebrate your differences, find out if they are strengths, and if so, nurture them.

Ask 3 people who know you very well what it is about you that makes you unique. What do they consider your stand-out qualities or features? Are they the answers you expected? *If not, consider whether you are sufficiently living your values. Revisit Step 1.*

Practice Happiness 32
Focus on understanding the other person first

Learn to:
❖ Ask more open-ended questions when involved in a misunderstanding
❖ Clear your mind of judgments, expectations, and assumptions
❖ Look for the element of truth in the other person's words

1. First, calm yourself

Most importantly, when trying to resolve a misunderstanding with someone or trying to make sense of an emotionally turbulent situation you need to be in an emotionally good place yourself first. So remember to regularly check your breathing rate. If you sense that you are feeling anxious – stop, take 2 breaths or count to 10.

2. Ask questions

Encourage the other person to open up by asking simple prompting questions such as, "What would you like to talk about?", "How are you feeling?", "What have I done that made you feel that way?" Open-ended questions (what, how) requiring longer answers – and which supply you with more information and discussion points – are preferable to closed questions (why, did) that simply encourage yes-no answers.

3. Clear your mind of judgments, expectations, and assumptions

As the whole point of this concept is to get into the other person's shoes, refrain from coloring their comments with your own judgments or expectations. Resist the urge to compare your opinion to theirs. You want to be able to see the world through their eyes, not yours.

4. Listen and then paraphrase

Every now and then paraphrase back to the person what you think they are telling you and ask for clarification if necessary. This shows you are listening, lets them know you value their opinion, and gives them the opportunity to clarify what they are saying. Example paraphrase statements may include, "So let me make sure I understand you correctly. I believe you're saying that……. Is that right?"

5. Ask the person more questions

If you are unclear of the message ask more questions, "I'm not sure what you mean by this.... Could you explain that again for me?"

6. Look for an element of truth in their words

If the person is giving an opinion of your past behaviors or intentions remember to refrain from making judgments while you are listening to them. Your intention is to understand how *they* see you. Keep your mind open to the possibility that they may be correct or partly correct. And, if this occurs, communicate this to them. This admission on your part will help defuse any tension and will reveal your compassionate side encouraging the other person to reciprocate in kind.

Recall the last time you had a misunderstanding with someone. How could your behavior have contributed to the misunderstanding?

_____

_____

What did the other person's perspective of the situation teach you about yourself?

_____

_____

Extra Resources

Bolton, R. (1986). *People skills: How to assert yourself, listen to others, and resolve conflicts.* New York, NY: Touchstone.

Goulston, M. (2009). *Just listen: Discover the secret of getting through to absolutely anyone.* New York, NY: AMACOM.

Sande, K. (2011). *Resolving everyday conflict.* Grand Rapids, MA: Baker Books.

> ## Practice Happiness 33
> *Look for the positive intention behind a person's behavior*
>
> ### Learn to:
> ❖ See a person's good qualities
> ❖ Separate the person from their behavior
> ❖ Appreciate that everyone may have different
>   positive intentions

1. Start with the assumption that the person is a good person

Before you can consider a person's positive intention you need to dispel any negative pre-judgments you may have about them. One way to do this is to make a concerted effort to look for the person's good qualities. Qualities might include behaviors such as the way they smile at people, the way they always hold the door open for others, their energy, their good hygiene practices. Or perhaps their self-discipline, their loyalty to friends, their respect for the environment. Or maybe their clothing style, their groovy rainbow-color shoes. Everyone has appealing, and even redeemable qualities. If you look for the good in a person, you'll find it. A side benefit is that others will begin to notice your own good qualities too.

Think of 3 people in you are not friends with. What appealing qualities does each of these people possess?

_____

_____

2. Separate the person from their behavior

This statement assumes that if someone fails at a task or their behavior doesn't match up to expectations, it is their behavior that may be at fault, not their personality. Behaviors are redeemable and can be changed, whereas labeling a person as "bad" condemns them as permanently broken. If you have to criticize someone, criticize the person's behavior and not the person.

3. Realize that everyone may have different positive intentions

Everyone has their own unique needs and perceptions of how to satisfy those needs depending on their backgrounds and values. Four smokers may each have a different positive intention for maintaining their habit. One may smoke for the physiological nicotine rush, one for stress relief, a third to hang with the crowd for the feeling of camaraderie, and another for the thrill of breaking rules. Knowing this becomes particularly important later on if a person wishes to change a particular behavior. Once a person's positive intention is established, work can begin to substitute an undesirable behavior with a more desirable behavior that fulfills the same intention.

Recall a recent moment when you saw someone doing something that baffled you. What were they doing and, giving them the benefit of the doubt, what might have been their positive intention?

_____

_____

4. Operate with a sense of compassion

When trying to identify a person's positive intention – the reason for their behavior – focus on giving them the benefit of doubt. Hold back any pre-judgments you may be tempted to form. Instead, try and step into their shoes to see the situation from their angle. What type of day or week have they had? What relationship troubles or work difficulties are they wrestling with? All of these things will probably impact upon their choice of behavior. Practice compassion.

The next time you find yourself having an argument with someone about something they did follow these steps: one, ask them to explain why they did what they did; two, explain to them your perceptions of their actions and how you arrived at those perceptions; three, listen to their explanation through their eyes, not yours (do not make any assumptions about their behaviors or any generalizations about their personality); four, choose whether to accept their explanation or not (but make your decision based on the specific behavior under discussion and not other issues).

Acknowledgments

I have been blessed to have had my life touched by so many people who – most without even realizing it – have each contributed to my personal understanding of this wonderful thing we call happiness. While almost every person I have bumped into on my travels or swapped greetings with at the local coffee shop has been one of my happiness teachers, there are certain people who deserve special mention.

The greatest thank you to my mother and father who constantly encouraged my sisters and I when we were youngsters to be true to ourselves and to live from the inside out.

To my three sisters for their unfailing emotional support and never-ending laughter a hearty thanks. They are true practitioners of living with a positive attitude. I love you more than words can express.

To Patti Korn for being brave enough to accompany me on an MGB road trip where she proofread the manuscript and kept me motivated I am indebted to you.

To Wayne Larkin whose creative genius developed the cover design of the book and who was a marvelous sounding board throughout the project a big thank you.

To Ryan Lee-Taylor from Blue Dog Cartoons for his clever caricature illustration and icons that required thinking outside of the box thank you.

And to all the people, and creatures, who played a role in revealing the happiness secrets within this book a big thank you. And please, just keep doing what you are doing.

About the Author

Bruce Wells, Ph.D, is a wellness expert who specializes in showing people how to enjoy happier lives by changing their behaviors and thought patterns, and by taking greater responsibility for everything that they do.

With a doctorate in stress management and degrees in health promotion and physical education he has worked in the wellness and motivation industries for 20 years offering services to elite athletes, corporate clients, university students, school teachers, and community groups. For two of these years he worked in China with business leaders and for five years he was based in Saudi Arabia offering wellness consultancy services to a major oil company and to tertiary education students and faculty.

Bruce has a diverse background in education having worked as a motivation speaker, primary school teacher, international tour guide, and shipwreck scuba dive instructor. He uses all of these experiences to provide presentations that are entertaining, inspirational, provocative, and, most of all, fun.

Based in Melbourne, Australia, Bruce speaks at conferences and conducts 1-hour, half-day, and full-day workshops with community, business, and school groups on topical issues including:

- Happiness Anywhere Anytime
- Principles of Personal Excellence
- Managing Stress Anywhere Anytime
- Work-Life Harmony
- Total Engagement Anywhere Anytime
- Healthy Habits Anywhere Anytime
- Communication Skills Plus Anywhere Anytime

For more information on these services visit Bruce's website at: **www.drbruce.com.au**